my revision notes

Edexcel AS/A-level

POLITICS
UK GOVERNMENT AND POLITICS

Neil McNaughton

Series Editor: Eric Magee

HODDER
EDUCATION
AN HACHETTE UK COMPANY

Acknowledgements

Every effort has been made to trace all copyright holders, but if any have been inadvertently overlooked, the Publishers will be pleased to make the necessary arrangements at the first opportunity.

Although every effort has been made to ensure that website addresses are correct at time of going to press, Hodder Education cannot be held responsible for the content of any website mentioned in this book. It is sometimes possible to find a relocated web page by typing the address of the home page for a website in the URL window of your browser.

Hachette UK's policy is to use papers that are natural, renewable and recyclable products and made from wood grown in sustainable forests. The logging and manufacturing processes are expected to conform to the environmental regulations of the country of origin.

Orders: please contact Bookpoint Ltd, 130 Park Drive, Milton Park, Abingdon, Oxon OX14 4SE. Telephone: (44) 01235 827720. Fax: (44) 01235 400401. Email education@bookpoint.co.uk Lines are open from 9 a.m. to 5 p.m., Monday to Saturday, with a 24-hour message answering service. You can also order through our website: www.hoddereducation.co.uk

ISBN: 978-1-4718-8966-0

© Neil McNaughton 2017

First published in 2017 by

Hodder Education,
An Hachette UK Company
Carmelite House
50 Victoria Embankment
London EC4Y 0DZ

www.hoddereducation.co.uk

Impression number   10 9 8 7 6 5 4 3

Year   2021 2020 2019 2018

Cover photo Tim Ellis/Alamy

Typeset in Bembo Std Regular 11/13 by Integra Software Services Pvt. Ltd., Pondicherry, India

Printed in India

A catalogue record for this title is available from the British Library.

Get the most from this book

Everyone has to decide his or her own revision strategy, but it is essential to review your work, learn it and test your understanding. These Revision Notes will help you to do that in a planned way, topic by topic. Use this book as the cornerstone of your revision and don't hesitate to write in it — personalise your notes and check your progress by ticking off each section as you revise.

Tick to track your progress

Use the revision planner on pages 4–7 to plan your revision, topic by topic. Tick each box when you have:

● revised and understood a topic
● tested yourself
● practised the exam questions and gone online to check your answers and complete the quick quizzes

You can also keep track of your revision by ticking off each topic heading in the book. You may find it helpful to add your own notes as you work through each topic.

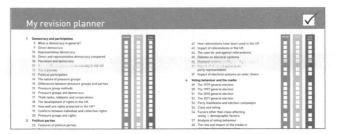

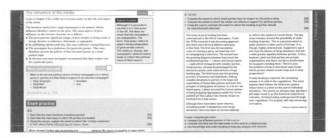

Features to help you succeed

Exam tips

Expert tips are given throughout the book to help you polish your exam technique in order to maximise your chances in the exam.

Typical mistakes

The author identifies the typical mistakes candidates make and explains how you can avoid them.

Now test yourself

These short, knowledge-based questions provide the first step in testing your learning. Answers are at the back of the book.

Definitions and key words

Clear, concise definitions of essential key terms are provided where they first appear.

Key words from the specification are highlighted in bold throughout the book.

Revision activities

These activities will help you to understand each topic in an interactive way.

Exam practice

Practice exam questions are provided for each topic. Use them to consolidate your revision and practise your exam skills.

Summaries

The summaries provide a quick-check bullet list for each topic.

Online

Go online to check your answers to the exam questions and try out the extra quick quizzes at **www.hoddereducation.co.uk/ myrevisionnotesdownloads**

My revision planner

REVISED   TESTED   EXAM READY

Now test yourself answers

Exam practice answers and quick quizzes at
www. hoddereducation.co.uk/myrevisionnotesdownloads

Countdown to my exams

6–8 weeks to go

- Start by looking at the specification — make sure you know exactly what material you need to revise and the style of the examination. Use the revision planner on pages 4–7 to familiarise yourself with the topics.
- Organise your notes, making sure you have covered everything on the specification. The revision planner will help you to group your notes into topics.
- Work out a realistic revision plan that will allow you time for relaxation. Set aside days and times for all the subjects that you need to study, and stick to your timetable.
- Set yourself sensible targets. Break your revision down into focused sessions of around 40 minutes, divided by breaks. These Revision Notes organise the basic facts into short, memorable sections to make revising easier.

REVISED ☐

2–6 weeks to go

- Read through the relevant sections of this book and refer to the exam tips, exam summaries, typical mistakes and key terms. Tick off the topics as you feel confident about them. Highlight those topics you find difficult and look at them again in detail.
- Test your understanding of each topic by working through the 'Now test yourself' questions in the book. Look up the answers at the back of the book.
- Make a note of any problem areas as you revise, and ask your teacher to go over these in class.
- Look at past papers. They are one of the best ways to revise and practise your exam skills. Write or prepare planned answers to the exam practice questions provided in this book. Check your answers online and try out the extra quick quizzes at **www.hoddereducation.co.uk/ myrevisionnotesdownloads**
- Use the revision activities to try out different revision methods. For example, you can make notes using mind maps, spider diagrams or flash cards.
- Track your progress using the revision planner and give yourself a reward when you have achieved your target.

REVISED ☐

One week to go

- Try to fit in at least one more timed practice of an entire past paper and seek feedback from your teacher, comparing your work closely with the mark scheme.
- Check the revision planner to make sure you haven't missed out any topics. Brush up on any areas of difficulty by talking them over with a friend or getting help from your teacher.
- Attend any revision classes put on by your teacher. Remember, he or she is an expert at preparing people for examinations.

REVISED ☐

The day before the examination

- Flick through these Revision Notes for useful reminders, for example the exam tips, exam summaries, typical mistakes and key terms.
- Check the time and place of your examination.
- Make sure you have everything you need — extra pens and pencils, tissues, a watch, bottled water.
- Allow some time to relax and have an early night to ensure you are fresh and alert for the examinations.

REVISED ☐

1 Democracy and participation

What is democracy in general?

REVISED

Before considering direct and representative democracy you should understand what the term 'democracy' means in its broadest sense. The following are commonly included criteria and can serve as a working definition when answering questions about democracy in general:

- The people have **influence**, either direct or indirect, over political decisions.
- Government and all elected bodies or individuals are made **accountable** to the people.
- Government should operate within the **rule of law**, whereby all are equal under the law and government itself is subject to the same laws as the people.
- **Elections** should be held regularly, be free and fair, and there should be universal adult suffrage.
- **People should be free** to form political parties and other associations and to stand for elective office.
- The **transition of power** from one government to the next must be peaceful.
- The people should have access to **independent information** and opinion.
- The **rights and freedoms** of the people should be respected by government.

Direct democracy

REVISED

The characteristics of **direct democracy** are as follows:

- The people make key decisions themselves.
- Only in classical Greece has a whole system been described as direct democracy.
- In its modern form, direct democracy uses initiatives and referendums.
- The UK is a representative democracy that uses direct democracy to resolve constitutional issues.

> **Direct democracy** A political system where the people themselves make political decisions. The modern equivalent is the use of referendums and initiatives within representative democracies.

Typical mistake

The term 'direct democracy' is not the same as 'referendum'. A direct democracy is a system where the people make all key decisions themselves. Such systems operated in classical Greece but are now rare and largely confined to small-scale communities. Referendums are really only examples of a direct democratic method, sometimes used within representative democracies.

Representative democracy

The characteristics of **representative democracy** are as follows:
- The people elect representatives to make political decisions on their behalf.
- Regular elections are a key feature.
- The system is characterised by representative assemblies such as parliaments, assemblies and councils.
- A government is elected to make key proposals and arrange for their implementation.
- Government and elected representatives are accountable to the people.
- Parties campaign to be able to represent the people in government.
- Pressure groups operate, representing sections of society and various causes from outside the political system.

> **Representative democracy**
> A political system based on the principle that the citizens elect representatives who make decisions on their behalf and are accountable to them. It can also refer to representation by political parties and by pressure groups.

Direct and representative democracy compared

Table 1.1 outlines a comparison between the two types of democracy.

Table 1.1 A comparison between direct and representative democracy

Advantages of direct democracy	Advantages of representative democracy
It is rule by the majority.	Representatives can protect minorities against rule by the majority.
It is the purest form of democracy. Direct democracy gives decisions **legitimacy**.	Representatives may have more knowledge and judgement than the mass of the people and are less likely to be swayed by emotion.
The people should respect decisions to which they have directly consented.	The people should respect decisions made by those with superior judgement and knowledge.
The so-called 'wisdom of crowds' suggests that large numbers of people will reach measured decisions.	People may not understand complex issues while elected representatives may be more understanding and reflective.
Decisions made by the people are entrenched (protected) and so cannot be easily overturned.	Elected representatives can be sensitive to changing situations.

> **Legitimacy** A term connected to democracy. It describes a situation where a decision is legitimate because it has been made democratically or by representatives if they have been democratically elected.

Pluralism and democracy

The term 'pluralism' implies the following aspects of a society and a political system:
- Power and influence are widely dispersed among the people and among sections of society — power is not excessively concentrated in a few hands.
- There is tolerance, both legal and cultural, of a wide range of minorities, political beliefs, religions, lifestyles and cultures.
- Political parties are free to operate and campaign and there are many parties which citizens may choose to support.

- Pressure groups and campaign groups are tolerated and allowed to operate freely.
- There is a range of sources of independent information, news and opinion available to the people without interference by the state.

> **Pluralist democracy** A description of a political system and/or society where there is widespread tolerance of different groups and lifestyles, where freedom of expression and association are respected, where many parties and pressure groups may operate and where there are independent media. The term also implies that power is dispersed and not concentrated.

> **Typical mistake**
>
> When asked to describe pluralism, students often confine themselves to saying that there are many parties and pressure groups and any citizens may stand for office. The terms 'pluralism' and '**pluralist democracy**' have much wider connotations, as described in this section.

An overall assessment of democracy in the UK

REVISED

Table 1.2 offers an assessment of UK democracy. The column headed 'Negatives' summarises the **democratic deficit** in the UK as described by many critics.

> **Democratic deficit** A term used to describe the senses in which democracy in the UK is flawed. The term 'deficit' implies that these flaws could be corrected through democratic reforms.

Table 1.2 Democracy in the UK — an assessment

Democratic feature	Positives	Negatives
Peaceful transition of power	The UK is remarkably conflict free.	None.
Free elections	Virtually everyone over the age of 18 can vote. There is little electoral fraud and there are strong legal safeguards.	The House of Lords is not elected at all, nor is the head of state (monarch).
Fair elections	There are proportional systems in place in Scotland, Wales and Northern Ireland and for European parliamentary elections.	The first-past-the-post system for general elections leads to disproportionate results and many wasted votes. Governments are elected on a modest proportion of the popular vote.
Widespread participation	There is extensive membership of pressure groups, which are free and active. There is also a growing level of participation in e-democracy.	Despite a small increase in turnout in the 2017 general election and an increase in party membership, both voter turnout and party activism remain rather low compared with the past.
of expression	The press and broadcast media are free of government interference. Broadcast media maintain political neutrality. There is free access to the internet.	Much ownership of the press is in the hands of a few large, powerful companies, such as News International.
Freedom of association	There are no restrictions on legal organisations. The UK is a pluralist society that tolerates many different groups, beliefs, lifestyles, religions and political movements.	Some associations are banned but this is because they are seen as being based on terrorism or racial hatred.

→

Democratic feature	Positives	Negatives
Protection of rights and liberties	This is strong in the UK. The country is signed up to the European Convention on Human Rights (ECHR) and the courts enforce it. The House of Lords protects rights, as does the judiciary.	Parliament is sovereign, which means rights are at the mercy of a government with a strong majority in the House of Commons. The ECHR is not binding on the UK Parliament.
The rule of law	This is upheld strictly by the judiciary. The right to judicial review underpins this. The judiciary is independent and non-political.	None.
Limited government and constitutionalism	Parliament and the courts ensure the government acts within the law.	There is no codified constitution so the limits to government power are vague. Parliamentary sovereignty means the government's powers could be increased without a constitutional safeguard. The prerogative powers of the prime minister are extensive and arbitrary.

Typical mistake

When assessing the state of democracy in the UK students often confine themselves to institutions — the House of Lords, the electoral system, the monarchy and the royal prerogative, typically. However, the test of democracy should be more widely considered to include such issues as how much political participation there is, how much pluralism flourishes (see 'Pluralism and democracy', above), whether there are free media and how widely dispersed power is.

Now test yourself

TESTED

1 Look at the following problems with democracy in the UK. In each case identify what measure or measures have been proposed to rectify the deficiency.

Democratic problem	Proposed remedy (remedies)
Part of the legislature is not accountable.	
The representation of parties in Parliament is distorted.	
There are often low turnouts at elections.	
There is a participation crisis in the UK.	

2 Outline three features of direct democracy.
3 Outline three features of pluralist democracy.

Answers on p. 122

The franchise

The **franchise** refers to the 'right to vote'. It has been fought for over many centuries but the UK currently enjoys 'universal adult suffrage'. The principles of UK **suffrage** are as follows:

- Everyone over the age of 18 has the right to vote in elections, save for a limited few such as convicted prisoners, the certified insane and members of the royal family.
- No groups are discriminated against in electoral law.
- It is the responsibility of each individual to register to vote.

Franchise issues

Issues concerning the extent of the franchise and the way UK citizens vote include the following:

- To combat low turnouts some advocate compulsory voting.
- Reducing the voting age to 16 has been proposed and was temporarily implemented in the 2014 referendum on Scottish independence.
- Online voting has been suggested, although there are problems with security.
- Weekend voting may make voting easier and increase opportunities to do so.

> **Franchise or suffrage** Both terms essentially mean the right to vote. In modern democracies suffrage is extended to all adults, with no groups excluded. It is unusual in a democracy for any group to be excluded from voting, so much so that a system which does exclude some or all citizens from voting cannot be described as democratic.

Political participation

The following are forms of political participation:

- voting in elections
- joining a political party
- becoming an *active* member of a party
- standing for election to office
- joining a pressure group
- becoming *active* in a pressure group
- taking part in a political campaign online or on the ground
- signing a petition or e-petition.

The participation crisis

Table 1.3 shows examples of the so-called **participation crisis** and the ways that have been proposed to counteract it.

> **Participation crisis** A description of the ways in which critics have suggested various forms of political participation may be declining in the UK, leading to a possible democratic crisis.

Table 1.3 Aspects of the 'participation crisis' and proposals to counteract it

Examples of falling participation	Proposals to remedy the problem
Low turnout at elections, especially among the young	Compulsory voting. Online voting. More political education in schools.
Political apathy	Increased use of referendums to engage more people in political debate.
Falling party membership	Electoral reform making more parties electable. Reduce party subscriptions (as Labour did in 2015).

Examples of falling participation	Proposals to remedy the problem
Disillusionment with politicians and political parties	A change in the electoral system might encourage support for smaller parties and independent candidates.
Shallow engagement with political issues ('slactivity') as a result of social media and online campaigns	More political education and politicians encouraging direct consultation with citizens.

Exam tip

When answering questions about ways in which the participation crisis might be solved or how democracy in the UK may be improved, it is important that you do not merely *describe* the changes proposed but also *explain why* they might work. For example, *why* might political education improve participation, *why* might the introduction of proportional representation improve election turnout?

Possible reasons why turnout at elections is falling include:

- disillusionment with political parties, especially among younger people, and a falling commitment to parties (partisan dealignment)
- people being more concerned with single issues than with broad policies
- a lack of distinction between the parties since the 1990s
- the electoral system results in large numbers of wasted votes (for smaller parties and in safe seats) and votes of unequal value (marginal versus safe seats). It also results in disproportional results
- with the emergence of referendums, voters prefer direct democracy.

Exam tip

The examiners will be looking for evidence of *synopticity*. This is linking descriptions and analysis from different parts of the specification. In the case of participation, you should include evidence from Chapter 4 about voting behaviour, electoral turnout and partisan dealignment.

The nature of pressure groups

REVISED

Table 1.4 outlines the features of pressure groups.

Table 1.4 Features of pressure groups

Promotional groups	Sectional groups
They are altruistic in that they serve the whole community, not just their own members and supporters.	They are largely (not always) self-interested in that they serve the interests of their own members and supporters.
They tend to concentrate on mobilising public opinion and putting pressure on government in that way.	Though they seek public support, they tend to seek *direct* links with decision makers (insider status).
They often use 'direct action' in the form of public demonstrations, internet campaigns and sometimes civil disobedience.	Their methods tend to be more 'responsible' and they often take the parliamentary route to influence.
They seek very widespread support.	They usually have a formal membership.

Differences between pressure groups and parties

The following differences should be noted:
- Parties seek to gain power or a share of power whereas pressure groups do not seek governmental power.
- Parties have to make themselves accountable to the electorate whereas pressure groups are not accountable except to their own members.
- Parties develop policies across all or most areas of government responsibility whereas pressure groups usually have narrower concerns and sometimes are concerned with only one issue.
- Parties usually have a formal membership and some kind of formal organisation whereas pressure groups often have supporters rather than members and sometimes have loose organisation.

Pressure group methods

Important examples of pressure group methods include the following (with examples of groups typically using such methods):
- **Lobbying.** This is direct contact with important decision makers, policy makers and legislators. Sometimes professional lobby organisations may be used. The method largely involves persuasion. It is used largely by insider groups, such as the National Farmers' Union (NFU), British Bankers' Association (BBA) and Confederation of British Industry (CBI). 'Mass lobbying' of Parliament is also used. Example: Age UK on behalf of pensioners.
- **Public campaigning.** This involves large-scale demonstrations of support for an issue or a group. It is designed to mobilise public opinion and show the level of support to decision makers. Examples: environmental groups, hospital doctors and nurses, teachers.
- **Donations to political parties.** These are legal as long as they are declared. They are typically used by large corporations and employer organisations or by trade unions.
- **Media campaigns.** These often feature celebrities and mobilise public support. Examples: Justice for Gurkhas (Joanna Lumley) and resources and a higher profile for mental health care (royal princes Harry and William).
- **Civil disobedience.** When other methods have failed, illegal methods may be used. Examples: Greenpeace (destroying GM crops), Animal Liberation Front (attacks on animal testing laboratories).
- **Social media and e-petitions.** Social media can be used to raise awareness (animal welfare groups) and gain support, to organise e-petitions (anti-fracking, anti-airport expansion) and local action.
- **Legal action.** Judicial reviews aim to prevent discrimination against women and minorities. Examples: the LGBT community, asylum seekers, women in employment.

> **Exam tip**
>
> It is very important always to try to describe and evaluate recent change in your answers. This is especially true of questions about pressure groups. The ways in which people try to influence decision makers is changing, especially in the digital age. You should be aware that the traditional methods of pressure groups are evolving into more direct forms of influence.

Changes in pressure group methods

New methods include:
- online campaigns
- write-in campaigns to MPs and other elected representatives
- e-petitions
- local action using 'flash demonstrations'
- use of the Human Rights Act to protect minority interests.

Pressure groups and democracy

The question is, do pressure groups threaten democracy or do they enhance it? See Table 1.5.

Table 1.5 Assessing whether pressure groups enhance or threaten democracy

Pressure groups enhance democracy	Pressure groups may threaten democracy
They help to disperse power and influence more widely.	Some groups are elitist and tend to concentrate power in the hands of too few people.
They educate the public about important political issues.	Influential groups may distort information in their own interests.
They give people more opportunities to participate in politics without having to sacrifice too much of their time and attention.	Those that are *internally undemocratic* may not accurately represent the views of their members and supporters.
They can promote and protect the interests and rights of minorities.	Finance is a key factor in political influence so groups that are wealthy may wield a disproportionate amount of influence.
They help to call government to account by publicising the effects of policy.	

Key examples of groups and action

There are various ways in which pressure groups may exert influence, as illustrated in Table 1.6.

Table 1.6 How pressure groups influence government

Type of group	Example	Nature of pressure
Insider pressure groups	Age UK	Close links with decision makers, lobbying ministers and Parliament, participation in policy committees.
Outsider pressure groups	Greenpeace	Demonstrations of public support, publicity campaigns, civil disobedience, digital campaigning.
Social movements	Occupy	Demonstrations, civil disobedience, online campaigning including e-petitions.
Single-issue campaigns	Against a third Heathrow runway	Illegal obstruction of the airport, digital campaigns, media representatives including celebrities, lobbying Parliament, recruiting sympathetic local MPs.
Trade unions and professional associations	British Medical Association	Strikes, non-cooperation and demonstrations, lobbying Parliament, using sympathetic MPs.
Companies and industries	Starbucks	Negotiating with government for favourable treatment.

Now test yourself

4 Look at the following forms of representation. In each case write in the kind of individual or body who might carry out this kind of representation.

Form of representation	Individual or body
Representing the interests of a locality	
Representing the national interest	
Representing the interests of a particular section of society	
Representing the interests of a social class	

5 Outline three features of representative democracy.

Answers on p. 122

Think tanks, lobbyists and corporations

There are various examples of **think tanks** which may influence policy.

Neutral think tanks

ResPublica — general policy issues.

Chatham House — international affairs.

Centre for Social Justice — policy on welfare issues.

Demos — current political issues.

'Left-wing' think tanks

Fabian Society — issues mainly concerning social justice and equality.

Institute for Public Policy Research — various left-wing policy ideas.

'Right-wing' think tanks

Adam Smith Institute — promoting free market solutions to economic issues.

Centre for Policy Studies — promoting ideas popular in the premiership of Margaret Thatcher.

'Liberal' think tanks

Liberty — promoting issues concerning the protection of rights and liberties.

Reform — concerning policies on welfare, public services and economic management.

> **Lobbyists** Professionals who are employed to lobby government to try to persuade decision makers to favour a particular group or cause. They may be individuals or companies and are often employed by businesses, employer groups, pressure groups, professional associations, trade unions and even foreign governments.
>
> **Think tank** The name given to an organisation set up to develop public policy or to lobby decision makers in the hope that they will adopt policies in a particular political direction. Usually staffed by academics, they have a variety of sources of funding, including business groups, universities, trade unions, political parties and even government itself.

Now test yourself

6 Identify an example of a particular pressure group or other association which might carry out the function and use the methods described.

Description	Example
An organisation that seeks to mobilise public opinion through the use of mass demonstrations	
An organisation that operates on behalf of business and seeks to influence ministers and parliamentarians directly	
An organisation that tends to use illegal methods or civil disobedience to gain public attention	
An organisation that has local concerns and typically uses social media to organise protest	
An organisation that uses insider status to represent the interests of a particular section of society	

7 Identify the differences between pressure groups and political parties.

Answers on p. 122

The development of rights in the UK

What are the sources of rights in the UK? The following examples show where our rights have come from:

● **Common law.** This has developed over many centuries. These are rights which have been recognised as existing and commonly enforced. They are confirmed by judicial precedent — judgments made in the courts and enforced by lower courts. Examples: the rule of law guaranteeing equal treatment under the law, habeas corpus (freedom from imprisonment without trial), rules relating to a fair trial.
● **Statutes.** Parliamentary law may guarantee rights. Examples: the Freedom of Information Act 2000 (granting the right to access official information), the Equality Act 2010 (guaranteeing freedom from unfair discrimination).
● **The Human Rights Act**. This brought the European Convention on Human Rights into UK law. A wide range of rights and freedoms are guaranteed.
● **European Union law (until 2019).** This guaranteed a wide range of social and economic laws. These will probably lapse when the UK leaves the EU.

Typical mistake

Many students mistakenly believe that the European Convention on Human Rights is controlled by the European Union. This would imply that when the UK leaves the EU, all these rights will be lost. This is not so. The ECHR is administered by a different body, the Council of Europe, and its European Court of Human Rights. The rights in the ECHR will be retained after the UK exits the EU.

How well are rights protected in the UK?

Table 1.7 outlines how rights are protected in the UK.

Table 1.7 An assessment of rights protection in the UK

Strengths	Weaknesses
There is a strong common law tradition.	Common law can be vague and disputed. It can also be set aside by parliamentary statutes.
The UK is subject to the European Convention on Human Rights.	Parliament remains sovereign and so can ignore the ECHR or can even repeal the Human Rights Act.
The judiciary has a reputation for being independent and upholding the rule of law even against the expressed wishes of government and Parliament.	There is increasing pressure on government, as a result of international terrorism, to curtail rights in the interests of national security. The right to privacy, the right of association and expression as well as freedom from imprisonment without trial are all threatened.
The principle of equal rights is clearly established.	

Conflicts between individual and collective rights

There are constant conflicts between the principle of individual rights and the rights of the community as a whole — see Table 1.8.

Table 1.8 Conflicts between individuals' rights and collective rights

Individual rights	Conflicting collective rights
Freedom of expression	The rights of religious groups not to have their beliefs satirised or questioned.
The right to privacy	The right of the community to be protected from terrorism by security services which may listen in on private communications.
The right to press freedom	The right of public figures to keep their private lives private.
The right to demonstrate in public places (right of association and free movement) and thus cause disruption	The right of the community to their own freedom of movement.
The right to strike in pursuit of pay and employment rights	The right of the community to expect good service from public servants who are paid from taxation.

Now test yourself

8 Identify the specific development that matches the purpose in relation to rights.

Purpose	Development (with date if applicable)
A piece of legislation guaranteeing a wide range of rights and liberties	
A piece of legislation giving citizens access to official documents and information	
The creation of a body which can act as the highest level of appeal when citizens feel their rights may have been abused or ignored	
A historical phenomenon stretching back centuries that guarantees anciently held rights	
A device that helps citizens to appeal against unfair or unequal treatment by public bodies	
A piece of legislation outlawing discrimination against women and minorities	

9 Describe three sources of rights in the UK.

Answers on p. 122–23

Pressure groups and rights

REVISED

There are a number of pressure groups concerned with rights in the UK. Prominent examples include the following:

- **Liberty:** probably the best-known group, it is a major campaigner and think tank.
- **Unlock Democracy:** this group is concerned with many constitutional reform issues, among which are methods of strengthening rights protection, including a codified constitution containing a bill of rights.
- **Amnesty International:** this is most concerned with the treatment of political prisoners abroad, but also concerns itself with the abuse of government power in the UK in the area of political rights.
- **The Fawcett Society:** this group campaigns for equal rights for women.
- **JUSTICE:** this is largely a lawyers' group campaigning for rights protection, especially in the area of law enforcement and trials.

Exam tip

When you are discussing rights the examiners will wish to see examples of how rights campaign groups are seeking to improve rights protection. It is worthwhile, therefore, quoting some examples of the work of the rights groups identified in this section.

Exam practice

AS

1 Describe the main features of direct democracy. [10]
2 Describe the main changes in the ways pressure groups have conducted
   campaigns in recent years. [10]
3 Using the source, explain the term 'participation crisis'. [10]

It has long been considered essential in any healthy democracy that there should be a high degree of political participation by citizens. Such participation ranges from the most basic type — voting in elections and referendums — to a much more intense form of involvement such as becoming active in support of a political party or even standing for office.

In the UK today, however, there are growing problems with participation. Turnout at most elections has been trending downwards and even some referendums have suffered from similarly low turnouts. At the same time membership of political parties has been steadily falling since the 1980s. This has been put down to a combination of political apathy, the perceived unfairness of the electoral system and a general growing disillusionment with party politics. People increasingly believe that the parties are too similar to each other and this makes voting at elections futile.

It is not all one-way traffic, however. Pressure groups have long since taken over many of the functions of parties in influencing decision makers. In more recent times, the growing use of the internet and social media has brought into political processes many more political activists. Nevertheless, many argue this is an unsatisfactory form of participation because it requires little effort and minimal knowledge to take part and so encourages minimal commitment.

If political participation continues to decline, critics argue, there is a danger that government will gain increasing power and cease to be accountable, and that power will become excessively concentrated into a few hands.

Source: original material

In your response you must use knowledge and understanding to analyse points that are only in the source. You will **not** be rewarded for introducing any additional points that are not in the source.

4 'Direct democracy is undoubtedly superior to representative democracy.'
   How far do you agree? [30]

A-level

1 Evaluate the extent to which the UK remains a genuine pluralist democracy. [30]
2 Evaluate the extent to which rights are effectively protected in the UK. [30]
3 Using the source, evaluate the view that representative democracy is
   superior to direct democracy. [30]

It is natural to assume that direct democracy is the purest form of political system that can exist. After all, it represents the ultimate form of government by consent and, at the same time, it means that the majority rules. It is also to be expected that the people are more likely to respect decisions they have made themselves. It does, however, have some illustrious critics. In classical Greece, the philosopher Plato argued that it would give rise to the rule of rabble-rousing dictators who would be able to sway opinion through great speeches and appeals to popular emotion. Today we see echoes of this in the way the tabloid press often treats referendum campaigns. In nineteenth-century England, the great liberal thinker John Stuart Mill referred to the 'tyranny of the majority' and, like Plato, feared that the average citizen, lacking much education, would not act rationally and would be ignorant of the issues presented to them. Mill and his fellow nineteenth-century liberals supported representative democracy. This was for several reasons.

First, they argued that elected representatives would be able to use their superior judgement in the interests of the people and would be able to arbitrate between the interests of the majority and those of minorities. Second, they believed that this compromise would satisfy the liberal desire to ensure that all sections of society are considered in political decision making.

→

Third, they had little faith in the people's ability to reach rational decisions.

It is hardly surprising, therefore, that representative democracy has now become the norm in modern liberal-based political systems. Nevertheless, there are now signs that direct democracy is creeping back into fashion. In the UK, considered to be the original cradle of representative democracy, governments are increasingly resorting to referendums, the modern form of direct democracy. Referendums are often used to settle constitutional issues and occasions when government itself is unable to resolve an issue without excessive conflict.

Source: original material

In your response you must:
● compare the different opinions in the source
● consider this view and the alternative to this view in a balanced way
● use knowledge and understanding to help you analyse and evaluate.

Answers and quick quiz 1 online

ONLINE

Summary

You should now have an understanding of:
● the distinction between direct and representative democracy
● the state of democracy in the UK — you will need at least three negative features and at least three positive features
● pressure groups — it is essential that you have contemporary examples to illustrate your analysis of their activities and the extent to which they have been successful
● the ways in which external groups seek to influence government and other decision makers — you must include examples of not only pressure groups but also think tanks, large corporations and **lobbyists**
● the status of rights in the UK — you will need plenty of examples of which rights are enforced and which are endangered.

2 Political parties

Features of political parties

REVISED

- Parties are associations of people who hold similar political views and wish to promote those views.
- Parties seek to gain governmental power at local, regional and national levels. The search for power distinguishes parties from other associations.
- Most parties have some kind of formal organisation, normally a hierarchy including leaders, activists and followers.
- Most parties have a system of membership.

Functions of political parties

REVISED

The main functions of political parties are to:

- develop policies and political programmes designed to solve problems in a society or to improve society
- select suitable candidates for office at all levels — local, regional and national
- identify and train political leaders, again at local, regional and national levels
- educate the public about important political issues
- provide organised opportunities for people to participate in politics
- when not in government, call the existing government to account.

Parties are an integral part of the UK political system — they help to organise elections and to run the business of representative bodies at local, regional and national levels.

> **Typical mistake**
>
> Students often confuse 'functions' with 'features' when looking at exam questions. Functions refers to what a body or association such as a party *does*, what its purposes are. Features refers to what it *looks like*, its main characteristics.

The funding of political parties

REVISED

Political parties have a number of different sources of finance, including:

- membership subscriptions
- fundraising events such as fetes, festivals, conferences and dinners
- donations from supporters
- loans from wealthy individuals or banks
- self-financing of candidates for office.

There is up to £2 million per party available in grants from the Electoral Commission, plus Short money, which grants funds to parties for research, depending on their size.

The proposals for reform of party funding include the following:

- Impose restrictions on the size of individual donations to parties. This is broadly the system used in the USA (though donors can grant funds to thousands of individual candidates). To be effective the cap would have to be relatively low.
- Impose tight restrictions on how much parties are allowed to spend. This would make large-scale fundraising futile.
- Restrict donations to individuals, e.g. outlaw donations from businesses, pressure groups and trade unions.

- Replace all funding with state grants for parties, paid for out of general taxation.

State funding is the most prominent proposal for reform. Table 2.1 shows the arguments in favour of and against the state funding of parties.

Table 2.1 The debate about state funding of parties

Arguments for	Arguments against
It will end the opportunities for the corrupt use of donations (often known as 'cash for honours'). Some donors give money in the expectation of being granted an honour.	Taxpayers may objective to funding what can be considered to be 'private' organisations. There are many other calls on government revenue which are seen as more important.
It will end the possibility of 'hidden' forms of influence through funding. Organisations and companies often deny they are seeking political advantage, but this claim is difficult to justify.	It will be difficult to know how to distribute funding. Should it be on the basis of past performance (in which case large parties will retain their advantage) or on the basis of future aspirations (which is vague)?
It will reduce the huge financial advantage that large parties enjoy and give smaller parties the opportunity to make progress.	Parties may lose some of their independence and will see themselves as organs of the state.
It will improve democracy by ensuring wider participation from groups that have no ready source of funds.	It may lead to excessive state regulation of parties.

Left wing and right wing

REVISED

Table 2.2 shows the main distinctions between **left-wing** and **right-wing** political ideas and ideals.

Table 2.2 Left- and right-wing political ideas

Left-wing ideas	Right-wing ideas
Redistributing income from rich to poor through taxation and welfare as well as a generous minimum wage.	Low levels of personal and corporate taxation to encourage private enterprise and create incentives to work.
Strong support for the welfare state and opposition to private-sector involvement in the provision of such services.	Acceptance of private-sector involvement in the provision of public services. Extreme right-wing views include the replacement of the welfare state with private insurance.
Support for workers' rights and trade union power and the protection of workers' rights in such areas as job security, fair contracts and good working conditions.	The state should not interfere with the working of the economy save for exceptional circumstances.
The state should support industries which are vital to society and the economy, typically energy, rail and the mail system.	Support for free markets in goods, finance and labour, including reducing trade union power.
Support for measures designed to create equality of opportunity, largely education.	Keeping welfare benefits relatively low as an incentive for people to find work and not become too dependent on the state.
A stress on equal rights for all groups in society, especially women and minorities.	A strong position on law and order.
Support for aid to poorer countries.	A stress on national unity and patriotism.

Left wing Ideologies, ideas and policies which tend towards socialism. Left wing refers to such ideas as redistribution of income, regulation of the excesses of capitalism, protection for workers' rights, a stress on state welfare and state control of some major industries.

Right wing A term related to ideologies, ideas and policies which tend towards the promotion of free market capitalism, acceptance of social and economic inequality and a limited role for the state. Typical policies include low taxation and welfare levels, the promotion of free markets, a hard line on crime and a preference for the collective rights of the community over individual human rights.

Table 2.3 places the political parties into the context of left–right ideas. The table includes the expressions 'centre-left' and 'centre-right'. These are useful expressions to replace 'moderate' left and right wing.

Table 2.3 Parties and the left–right spectrum

Party	Left–right position	Notes and exceptions
Conservative	Centre-right	There is a large right-wing minority in the party.
Labour	Left	The leadership group is left wing but many MPs are centre-left.
Liberal Democrat	Centre-left	Many party supporters are very centrist.
UKIP	Right	Some describe UKIP as extreme right. It does have some extremist supporters.
Green Party	Left	The party's main concern is environmentalism, but it has other left-wing views.
Scottish National Party	Centre-left	Independence is the main policy, but it is close to Labour in its other ideals.
Plaid Cymru	Centre-left	In non-nationalist policies it is similar to Labour.
DUP (Northern Ireland)	Right	Largely concerned with Northern Ireland domestic issues.

Now test yourself

1 Look at the policies described in the left-hand column. In each case state whether you think they are left wing, right wing or neither (i.e. centrist).

Policy	Left wing, right wing or centrist?
The nationalisation of the railways	
The raising of the minimum wage well above the rate of inflation or the increase in earnings	
Reducing the rate of corporation tax levied on businesses	
Extending the rights of workers against unfair employment practices	
Extending the construction of nuclear power stations	
Increasing the level at which people start paying inheritance tax to £1 million	
Transferring local authority services into the private sector	

2 Outline two other policies not mentioned above which could be described as right wing and two which could be described as left wing.

Answers on p. 123

You should distinguish between the following when looking at the policies of the parties:

- **Ideologies:** the very fundamental ideas and beliefs that underpin the development of parties.
- **Ideas:** the main political views of virtually all those who support the party.
- **Policies:** the policies adopted by the current leadership.

Typical mistake

Students often confuse party *ideas* with party *policies*. Party ideas are the main long-terms ideas that have tended to flourish within a party, whereas policies are the short-term proposals which the leadership of a party has developed. The policies of a party are mostly based on the dominant ideas of the party, but they are not the same thing.

Exam tip

It is vital that you combine your reading about political parties with your reading about political ideas when doing your revision. You need to relate the policies of the parties today to their ideological background to see the extent to which they have followed or moved away from those ideological roots.

The Conservative Party

Ideology

- A stress on order and harmony in society (**one nation**).
- Opposition to strongly held ideology or political principles.
- A preference for gentle reform over radical ideas.
- A belief in individualism and a limited state.
- Support for traditional institutions and values.
- Nationalism.

One nation Idea associated with many conservatives. It refers to ideas and policies designed to unite the country and which seek to avoid social conflict by ensuring that the wealthy in society are not allowed to exploit the poor.

Prominent ideas

- A pragmatic approach to political decision making.
- Low taxation.
- Financial responsibility.
- Stressing the importance of private property ownership.
- Support for capitalism.
- Preference for community rights over individual rights.
- Stress on law, order and national security.

Current policies

(Based on the June 2017 Queen's Speech outlining government policies for two years)

- To achieve a surplus government budget as soon after 2020 as possible.
- To renew the Trident nuclear submarine missile system.
- To negotiate the best possible terms for leaving the European Union.
- To increase the personal tax-free income tax allowance to £12,500 per annum.
- To reduce the tax burden on company profits.
- To reduce the tax burden on middle-income groups.
- Generous increases in the minimum wage by 2020.
- Not to increase the rate of VAT.
- To reduce tax avoidance and evasion by individuals and companies.
- To build a Northern Powerhouse by investing in infrastructure in northern England.
- Reform of the social care system to reduce the burden on low-income groups.

The Conservative party features the following important **party factions**:

- Thatcherism (**New Right**) — supporting the policies adopted in the 1980s. They include neo-liberal ideas of free markets, low taxation, low levels of welfare benefits and the weakening of trade unions plus neo-conservatism which wishes to see a strong, authoritarian state. The main group is called Conservative Way Forward.
- Liberal progressive conservatism — opposes the Thatcherite agenda and accepts the need for greater social justice, liberal policies towards lifestyles and a balanced view of welfare versus low taxation. The Tory Reform Group is the main example.
- One nation Tories — now a small minority who wish to avoid policies which may be socially divisive.
- Eurosceptics — after the UK's decision to leave the EU, this group hopes that the UK will not join the European single market or the European customs union but will claim full economic independence.

The Labour Party

REVISED

Ideology

- To reduce inequality in society.
- To regulate capitalism.
- A belief in the power of the state to promote social and economic reform.
- To balance the interests of workers against those of employers.
- To promote equal opportunities and reduce unjustified privilege.

Party faction A group within a political party, either formal or informal, which promotes ideas that are significantly different to the mainstream ideas of the party within which they reside.

New Right Ideas and policies associated with conservatism during the late 1970s and 1980s, led by Margaret Thatcher and US President Reagan. It is a combination of neo-liberalism, proposing free markets, the free operation of the private sector, no state intervention and reductions in levels of welfare, and neo-conservatism, which is nationalistic, opposed to excessive social diversity and takes a hard line on law and order.

Typical mistake

Be careful not to confuse the Conservative Party with 'conservatism' as a political movement. While most members of the party are also conservatives, not all conservatives are also members of the Conservative Party. Similarly, liberalism as an ideology and political movement is not entirely synonymous with the Liberal Democratic Party or any other Liberal party in the world.

Prominent ideas

- Support for an extensive, well-funded welfare state.
- A progressive tax system to redistribute real income.
- Relatively high direct taxes to fund public services.
- Support for a strong, free, comprehensive education system.
- The promotion of equal rights.
- Measures to reduce poverty, especially child poverty.

Current policies

(Based on the 2017 party manifesto)

- To increase taxation on the wealthiest groups in society.
- To increase taxation on company profits.
- To reduce taxation on low-income groups.
- To attack tax evasion and avoidance.
- Significant increases in the minimum wage.
- To reverse welfare benefit cuts implemented since 2010.
- To bring the railways, water companies and Royal Mail under public ownership (nationalisation).
- Large-scale government borrowing for capital spending on transport, schools and hospitals.
- To restore trade union powers removed since 2010.
- To increase spending on health and social care.
- To abolish university tuition fees.
- An extensive programme of affordable house building.

The Labour Party features the following important party factions:

- The supporters of Jeremy Corbyn, known as Momentum. They support left-wing socialist policies such as the re-nationalisation of some important industries and strong regulation of public utilities, strengthening trade unions, and raising taxes to redistribute income and improve welfare services. They are sometimes referred to as **Old Labour** or **democratic socialists**.
- The opponents of Corbyn and supporters of centrist policies such as poverty-reduction programmes, mild redistribution of income, support for the welfare state but not excessively generous state benefits, and a pragmatic approach to economic management. Sometimes they are referred to as **New Labour** supporters or even Blairites, or sometimes moderate **social democrats**.

Typical mistake

It is commonly believed that the British Labour Party was once a *socialist* party. This is not really true, though many members have been socialist or have referred to themselves as socialist. It is better to say that the Labour Party used to be *democratic socialist* in nature and in more recent times became *social democratic* under Blair. Under Corbyn it returned to a democratic socialist stance but was not pure socialist. Pure socialists will accept no compromise with capitalism.

Old Labour A title given to the ideas and policies of the Labour Party during the late 1970s and the 1980s. At that time most ideas and policies were left wing and could be described as democratic socialist in nature.

Democratic socialism A name given to a political movement, mostly within the Labour Party, that offers a compromise between capitalism and socialism and proposes interference with the economy in order to create more equality and a degree of state control over major industries.

New Labour A title given to the majority of Labour supporters from the mid-1990s onwards together with the ideas and policies associated with this group, which was led by such figures as Tony Blair, Peter Mandelson, Robin Cook and Gordon Brown. New Labour proposed a moderate form of social democracy also known as the 'third way'.

Social democracy A name given to a very moderate form of socialism that accepts the importance of capitalism and stresses individualism rather than equality.

The Liberal Democratic Party

Ideology

- Strong belief in individual liberty.
- Strong belief in equality of opportunity.
- Stress on equal rights and the rule of law.
- A belief in state welfare.
- Constitutional government to prevent abuse of power.

Prominent ideas

- Constitutional reform to make the UK more democratic and to decentralise power.
- The redistribution of income through tax and welfare.
- Greater protection for the environment and natural resources.
- Support for private property ownership.
- A strong, free, well-supported education system to promote equality of opportunity.
- The abolition of inherited privilege.

Current policies

(Based on the 2017 party manifesto)

- A proposal for a referendum on any final 'deal' negotiated by the government with the EU.
- Strong measures to protect the environment and to promote renewable sources of energy.
- Reignite the debate about constitutional issues such as electoral reform and an elected second chamber.
- A programme of building affordable housing.
- Reduce taxes on low-income groups.
- A vigorous attack on tax evasion and avoidance.
- Significant increases in the minimum wage.
- Large increases in spending on health, social care and education.
- Restoration of the pre-2010 levels of some welfare benefits.

The Liberal Democratic Party features the following important party factions:

- Most Liberal Democrats support centre-left policies similar to those adopted by the centrists in the Labour Party, together with a strong position on environmental control and constitutional reform. These are sometimes described as **modern liberals**.
- So-called Orange Book Liberals support constitutional reform and environmentalism but also support neo-liberal policies which would establish very free product, labour and financial markets. This is a throwback to their nineteenth-century predecessors known as **classical liberals**.

> **Modern liberals** Liberals who emerged after classical liberalism in the late nineteenth century. While still insisting on maximum freedom they also accept that the state should intervene to create greater equality of opportunity, welfare and social justice. Modern liberals also support social diversity.
>
> **Classical liberals** Liberals following a form of liberalism harking back to the nineteenth century which proposed the maximisation of personal freedom and the minimal state.

Exam tip

When looking at the parties' ideas and policies, remember to revise some of the party factions that do not conform to the conventional policies.

Revision activity

Revise the key distinctions between:
1 Old and New Labour.
2 One nation and New Right conservatism.
3 Liberalism and socialism.

The importance of other parties

REVISED

You should know the main political stance and impact of these parties:
- United Kingdom Independence Party (UKIP)
- Scottish National Party (SNP)
- Plaid Cymru (Welsh Nationalists)
- Green Party
- Democratic Unionist Party (DUP) (Northern Ireland conservatives)
- Sinn Fein (Northern Ireland Irish nationalists)

The ideas, policies and impacts of other parties

REVISED

Table 2.4 shows the broad political stance of small parties.

Table 2.4 The political stance of small parties in the UK

Party	Principal policy	General political stance
Scottish National Party	Scottish independence	Centre-left
UKIP	UK to leave the EU	Right
Green Party	Environmental protection	Left
Plaid Cymru	More self-government for Wales	Centre-left
Democratic Unionist Party	Close links between Northern Ireland and the UK	Right
Sinn Fein	Reunification of Ireland	Centre-left

Small and emerging parties in the UK can have the following impacts on the outcome of elections and on the three main parties:
- They may divert votes away from the main parties. Examples: the SNP has decimated Labour support in Scotland; UKIP took votes away from both the Conservatives and Labour in 2015.
- When a constituency is marginal between large parties, small parties may split the vote one way or the other. Example: the Green Party splits the centre-left vote.
- Small parties may affect the policies of large parties if they present an electoral threat. Example: UKIP has pushed the Conservative Party to take a harder line on negotiations with the EU.

> **Exam tip**
>
> Remember that the influence of small parties is not confined to how many seats they may win in representative assemblies. Small parties may threaten to win some of the votes normally cast for a large party. The policies of the large parties might be changed to head off this challenge.

The main policies of the small parties, based on the 2017 manifestos, include those shown in Table 2.5.

Table 2.5 Selected minor party policies (2017)

Party	Examples of policies
SNP	<ul><li>Scottish independence.</li><li>Failing independence, greater autonomous powers for Scotland within the UK.</li><li>Redistribution of income from rich to poor.</li><li>Strong support for public-sector health</li><li>and education.</li><li>Investment in renewable energy.</li><li>Cancellation of the Trident nuclear missile programme.</li></ul>
UKIP	<ul><li>Often described as **populism**.</li><li>UK to leave the European single market.</li><li>Strong controls over immigration.</li><li>Preference for British citizens in jobs, housing,</li><li> welfare and education.</li><li>An attack on companies that avoid and evade tax.</li><li>Reduced expenditure on overseas aid.</li></ul>
Plaid Cymru	<ul><li>Similar nationalist policies to the SNP but</li><li>acceptance that Welsh independence is unlikely</li><li>for many years.</li><li>Similar economic and social policies to the SNP.</li></ul>
Green Party	<ul><li>Strong controls on environmental damage and strict emissions control targets (**green politics**)</li><li>Very large investment in generation of renewable energy.</li><li>Radical redistribution of income from rich to poor.</li><li>Cancellation of the Trident nuclear missile programme.</li><li>Radical constitutional reform.</li></ul>
DUP*	<ul><li>Close ties between Northern Ireland and the rest of the UK.</li><li>Keeping an open border with the Republic of Ireland after Brexit.</li><li>Resistance to liberal social policies such as same-sex marriage.</li><li>Opposition to integration of religious schools.</li></ul>

* You are not required to have knowledge of Northern Ireland party policies, as their policies mostly relate to the province specifically.

> **Populism** A general name for ideas and policies designed to appeal to people who are disillusioned with conventional politics, who fear the loss of national identity and who wish to protect the economy from external competition. The policies of UKIP are a prime example.
>
> **Green politics** A general term relating to ideas and policies which are designed to protect the environment and to conserve natural resources.

Typical mistake

Although the Scottish National Party, Plaid Cymru and Sinn Fein are all nationalist parties, it is a mistake to assume they are defined *completely* by their nationalist aspirations. All three parties are also left of centre in their general political stance.

Now test yourself

3 Look at the following policies. With which party or parties would you associate these policies?

Policy	Party or parties
The introduction of more selective grammar schools	
The cancellation of the Trident nuclear missile renewal programme	
The reunification of Ireland	
The abolition of university tuition fees	
The introduction of proportional representation for general elections	
An extensive programme of infrastructure projects funded by government borrowing	
Strict controls on immigration into the UK	

4 Outline three policies of the Green Party not shared by the three main parties.
5 Identify three policies proposed by each of the following parties at the 2017 general election:
- Conservative Party
- Labour Party
- Liberal Democratic Party
- UKIP
- Scottish National Party

Answers on p. 123

The multi-party system

Table 2.6 summarises a number of **party system** descriptions.

Table 2.6 Party systems in the UK

Type	Description	Where it operates
Dominant party	One party dominates the number of seats in the legislative body.	The Scottish Parliament.
Two-party	Only two parties have significant representation.	In English constituencies.
Three-party	Three parties have significant representation.	After 2015 only three parties had a significant number of seats in the House of Commons — Conservative, Labour and the SNP.
Multi-party	Four or more parties have a significant number of representatives elected.	The Northern Ireland and Welsh assemblies plus many local government areas.

Party system A reference to how many parties achieve representation and have an influence on the politics of a country.

Tables 2.7 and 2.8 show the distinction between two-party dominance in terms of *seats* in the Westminster Parliament and the decline of two-party dominance in terms of *votes*.

Table 2.7 Two-party dominance in the UK in terms of parliamentary seats

Election year	Conservative seats	Labour seats	Third party seats	% of seats won by two main parties
1987	376	229	22	93.0
1992	336	271	20	93.2
1997	165	418	46	88.4
2001	166	413	52	87.8
2005	198	356	62	85.6
2010	307	258	57	86.9
2015	331	232	56	86.7
2017	318	262	35	89.2

Table 2.8 Decline in two-party dominance in votes (reversed 2017)

Election year	% of votes won by two main parties
1979	80.8
1983	70.0
1987	75.1
1992	77.5
1997	75.5
2001	72.4
2005	67.5
2010	65.1
2015	67.3
2017	80.4

Multi-party systems, however, thrive in the devolved assemblies and in local government:

- **Scotland:** a four/five-party system.
- **Wales:** a five-party system.
- **Northern Ireland:** a five-party system.
- **Local government:** two-, three- and four-party systems are all common.

> **Exam tip**
>
> When considering party systems in the UK, remember that the assemblies in Scotland, Wales and Northern Ireland have multi-party systems to a much greater extent than the Westminster Parliament. Local councils also often have multi-party systems.

> **Revision activity**
>
> Revise and remember the performance of the following parties in the last four general elections:
> 1 UKIP.
> 2 The Scottish National Party.
> 3 The Green Party.

Factors affecting party success

REVISED

Much of the material relating to the success or otherwise of parties is contained in Chapter 4 on voting behaviour. The following are key elements in parties' fortunes:

- **Quality of leadership:** this includes the following qualities which are known to attract support:
  - experience
  - decisiveness
  - ability to lead
  - media image
  - intelligence
  - apparent honesty.
- **Valence:** this refers to how people generally view the party's image. It includes such issues as:
  - How competent were they when they were last in office?
  - How economically responsible do they appear to be?
  - Are they trustworthy?
- **Unity:** parties that are disunited tend to fare badly at elections. The opposite is true: united parties are usually successful. There are positive and negative examples:
  - In 1983 and 1987 a divided Labour party was heavily defeated by a united Conservative Party under Margaret Thatcher.
  - In 1997 the Conservatives were divided over Europe and lost heavily to Labour, which was united around Tony Blair's New Labour agenda.
  - In 2015 the divided Liberal Democratic Party lost most of its seats in the UK Parliament.

> **Revision activity**
>
> Revise the impact of the image and reputation of the following leaders in terms their parties' fortunes in general elections:
> 1 Gordon Brown.
> 2 Ed Miliband.
> 3 Jeremy Corbyn.
> 4 Theresa May.

> **Exam tip**
>
> When looking at the success and failure of parties, you should also revise material in Chapter 4 on voting behaviour.

The influence of the media

Look at Chapter 4 for a fuller set of revision notes on the role and impact of the media.

The broadcast media have a legal requirement to be neutral. Media influence therefore centres on the press. The main aspects of press influence on the fortunes of parties are as follows:

- The press presents significant images of party leaders as being weak or strong, decisive or indecisive, charismatic or unpopular.
- By publishing opinion poll data, they may influence voting behaviour.
- The newspapers have preferences for particular parties. They may, therefore, present the policies of their favoured parties in a more positive light.
- At election time most newspapers recommend that their readers vote for a particular party.

> **Typical mistake**
>
> Although it is accurate to say there is a 'free press' in the UK, this does not mean that the newspapers are independent. The term 'free press' refers to papers being independent of government control. The reality is, though, that newspapers' political stance tends to reflect the political views of their owners.

Now test yourself

TESTED

6 What is the normal political stance of these newspapers (i.e. which party or parties are they likely to support in an election campaign)?
- *Daily Telegraph*
- *Daily Mail*
- *Daily Mirror*
- *Guardian*
- *Sun*

Answers on p. 123

Exam practice

AS

1 Describe the main functions of political parties. [10]
2 Describe the main ways in which UK parties are funded. [10]
3 Using the source, explain the extent to which the 'Corbyn revolution' in the Labour Party reflected typical Labour ideas. [10]

When Jeremy Corbyn was surprisingly but overwhelmingly elected Labour Party leader in 2015, following the resignation of Ed Miliband, many commentators called the event a 'revolution'. They argued that the ideas of Corbyn and his close supporters were actually a restoration of Labour Party ideas that had flourished in the 1970s and early 1980s. Policies such as the nationalisation of the railways, water companies and Royal Mail, indeed, took the party back to the 1940s. In addition, the party leadership proposed that there should be a major increase in taxes on the rich and vast increases in expenditure on health and education. Even more radically, Corbyn proposed to abolish tuition fees for university students, a measure that was designed to advance the cause of equality of opportunity. Even so, perhaps the expression 'back to the seventies' was an exaggeration. There was no full-scale attack on capitalism and the idea of centralised state planning was absent from the proposals. The party under Corbyn has believed in significant redistribution of income but not to the same extent as proposals put forward by Michael Foot in the 1980s.

Even so, compared with the moderate social democratic ideas of the party under Tony Blair, Gordon Brown and Ed Miliband, the Corbyn revolution was a radical departure. In the end a judgement on Corbyn's policies depends upon which Labour Party tradition one is comparing him with.

Source: original material

In your response you must use knowledge and understanding to analyse points that are only in the source. You will **not** be rewarded for introducing any additional points that are not in the source.

4 'The Conservative Party is now more a liberal party than a right-wing party.' How far do you agree with this view? [30]

A-level

1 Evaluate the extent to which small parties have an impact on UK politics today. [30]

2 Evaluate the extent to which the media can influence support for political parties. [30]

3 Using the source, evaluate the extent to which the funding of parties should be controlled and reformed. [30]

The issue of party funding has been controversial in the UK for many years. From the 1970s onwards it was becoming apparent that there were three problems emerging in this field. The first was the escalating costs of running a party, not least the cost of campaigning in elections. The second was the growing disparity between how much the established parties — Labour and Conservative — could afford compared with smaller parties. Small parties, already disadvantaged by the electoral system, now suffered from a huge funding gap. The third issue was the growing practice of business and individuals making sizeable donations to parties in the hope and expectation of favourable policies and even the prospect of being given an honour. In a tit-for-tat blame game, Labour accused the Conservatives of being bribed by big business while the Tories pointed out that Labour was heavily reliant on funding from trade unions.

Although there have been some reforms, including greater transparency over large donations, there has been no serious attempt to reform the system in recent times. The key issue revolves around the possibility of state funding of parties. This is a practice which is quite common in other parts of Europe. It is, though, highly controversial. Supporters say it will stop the abuses of large donations and will create greater equality between parties. Critics, however, point out that parties are private organisations and there can be no justification for taxpayers funding them. There is also the problem of how to distribute state funds: which parties should receive help and in what proportions?

If state funding is rejected, the remaining answer is to reform the regulations. The most popular idea follows the American system where there is a limit on the size of individual donations. This seems an obvious step, but there are ways round it, as the American experience indicates. Driving funding underground through over-regulation, it is argued, will only encourage corruption.

Source: original material

In your response you must:
- compare the different opinions in the source
- consider this view and the alternative to this view in a balanced way
- use knowledge and understanding to help you analyse and evaluate.

Answers and quick quiz 2 online

ONLINE

Summary

You should now have an understanding of:
- the ideologies and ideas of the main parties in the UK
- the contemporary policies of the main parties
- the policies of small and emerging parties
- both the functions and features of political parties in the UK
- the changing location of sovereignty in the UK
- the issues surrounding the funding of political parties
- the multi-party system
- the factors that determine the success or failure of parties
- the influence of the media on party fortunes.

3 Electoral systems

First-past-the-post (plurality system)

REVISED

The main features of first-past-the-post are as follows:
- The country is divided into constituencies.
- Each constituency returns one Member of Parliament (MP).
- At elections, each party presents one candidate.
- The winner of the election is the candidate who wins more votes than any other candidate. This is known as a **plurality**.
- It is not necessary to win an overall (more than 50%) majority to win a seat — about half the winning candidates in the UK do not gain more than 50% of the votes in their constituency.

The outcomes of first-past-the-post include the following:
- Many seats are **safe seats**. This means that the same party wins the seat at every election and there is no realistic possibility that any other party could win the seat. Only a minority of seats are **marginal seats**, which are seats where more than one party has a chance of winning.
- Usually the system tends to produce a result where a single party wins an overall majority of the seats in the House of Commons and can therefore govern without the support of members of other parties. However, this was not the case in 2010 and June 2017.
- Small parties have virtually no chance of winning seats.
- It is therefore associated with a two-party system.
- As each party must nominate a single candidate in each constituency, the system tends to favour the selection of candidates who are 'safe', i.e. mostly middle-class, straight white men.

> **Safe seat** A constituency where one party is so dominant that it is almost unthinkable that it will not win the seat at every election.
>
> **Marginal seat** A constituency where more than one party has a realistic chance of winning the seat at an election and the outcome of the election is likely to be close.

Now test yourself

TESTED

1 Outline three ways in which elections enhance democracy. Consider the following features:
- The mandate
- Legitimacy
- Accountability
- Representation

Answers on p. 124

The additional member system (hybrid system)

REVISED

This system (AMS) operates in elections to the Scottish Parliament, the Welsh Assembly and the Greater London Assembly. It is a hybrid between first-past-the-post and **proportional representation** (PR). It works like this:
- Two-thirds of the seats are elected using first-past-the-post, as for UK general elections.
- The other third of the seats are elected on the basis of closed regional list voting. The country is divided into regions and each party offers a

> **Proportional representation** A description of any electoral system that awards seats broadly in proportion to the votes cast for each party.

list of candidates for each region. Voters have two votes — one for the constituency and the other for one of the party lists. Seats are awarded to each party in the list system in proportion to the votes cast — the more votes, the more seats awarded.

- There is an important variation in the regional list part of the vote. The **variable top-up** system adjusts the proportions of votes cast on the list system. This is a complex calculation, but in essence what happens is that the seats awarded from the list system are adjusted to give a more proportional result. It is known as the D'Hondt method.
- Parties that do less well in the constituencies (typically Conservatives or Greens) have their proportion of list votes adjusted upwards. Those that do proportionally well under first-past-the-post (typically Labour) have their list votes adjusted downwards.
- The overall effect of variable top-up is to make the total result close to proportional of the total votes cast in both systems.

The outcomes of the additional member system include:
- The overall outcome tends to be approximately proportional to the votes cast.
- There are many safe constituency seats, so there are few violent swings in the seats won for each of the parties.
- Voters have two votes. A minority 'split the ticket' by voting for one party in the constituency vote but a different party in the list part of the system.
- Small parties can win seats even though they do not have a chance of winning any constituencies.

> **Variable top-up** A device used in the additional member system whereby the parties that are most discriminated against in the constituency system are awarded additional seats in the list system to compensate. The method helps to make the system more proportional.

The single transferable vote (proportional system)

REVISED

The single transferable vote (STV) system is used in Northern Ireland and in Scottish local government elections. It operates in this way:
- There are six seats available in each constituency.
- Each party is permitted to put up as many candidates as there are seats, i.e. up to six. In practice, parties do not adopt six candidates as they have no chance of winning all six seats available. Four is the normal maximum number from each party.
- Voters put the candidates in their order of preference by placing a number 1, 2, 3, etc. beside their names.
- Voters can vote for candidates from different parties or even all the parties, though few actually do.
- At the count an **electoral quota** is calculated. This is established by taking the total number of votes cast and dividing it by the number of seats available plus 1. So, if 50,000 votes were cast and six seats are available, the quota is $50,000 \div (6 + 1 = 7)$. This works out as 7,143. One is then added, giving a final figure of 7,144.
- At first all the first preferences are counted for each candidate. Any candidates who achieve the quota are elected automatically.
- After this stage the counting is complex. Essentially, the second and subsequent preferences from the ballot papers of the elected candidates are added to the other candidates. If this results in an individual achieving the quota, he or she is elected.
- This process continues until six candidates have achieved the quota and are elected.

The outcomes of the single transferable vote system include the following:

- The overall outcome is largely proportional to the first preference votes case for each party.
- It results in a multi-party system.
- Very small parties and independent candidates have a chance of winning seats.
- The fact that voters can discriminate between all the candidates and have many votes leads to candidates with greater social and demographic diversity being elected.

Now test yourself

TESTED

2 Consider the various arguments in favour of the introduction of proportional representation. Explain one way PR might favour each of the following:
- Proportionality
- Voter choice
- Equal value of votes
- Small parties
- Democratic legitimacy

Answers on p. 124

The supplementary vote (majority system)

REVISED

The supplementary vote system is used to elect single candidates. It is best known for being used to elect mayors in English cities and regions. It operates like this:

- Voters have two choices, a first and second choice. If any candidate achieves an overall majority, i.e. more than 50%, of the first choices in the first round, he or she is automatically elected.
- If this does not happen, the top two candidates go into a second round of counting. All the others drop out.
- The second-choice votes are added to the first choices to give two final totals. As there are only two candidates left, one of them must achieve an absolute majority.
- Therefore the winner has an overall majority of a combination of first- and second-choice votes.

The outcomes of the supplementary vote system include the following:

- The winner can claim to enjoy the support, either first or second choice, of an overall majority of the voters.
- It favours candidates from the major parties — small-party candidates have little chance of winning.
- Candidates' personality and perceived qualities are almost as important as their party allegiance.

Revision activity

Revise and remember the following:
1 The main impacts of the additional member system.
2 The main impacts of the single transferable vote system.
3 The reasons why the supplementary vote is used to elect single officials such as mayors.

Exam tip

Make absolutely sure you can efficiently describe the workings of all the electoral systems mentioned in the specification. If you know these descriptions well, it will save time in the exam.

Typical mistake

Many students confuse the *workings* of an electoral system with the *impact* of an electoral system. The workings describe how the system operates while the impact concerns the typical results and outcomes of a system. Be careful to read the wording of the question properly.

Now test yourself

3 Which electoral system is being described?

Description	Electoral system
An electoral system that regularly produced a government with a working majority in the UK Parliament until 2010	
An electoral system that allows voters to discriminate between candidates of the same party	
An electoral system that ensures that the winner is supported by a majority of voters	
An electoral system that gives voters two votes	
An electoral system that features both constituencies and proportional representation	

4 Describe the way in which the additional member system compensates parties that fare badly in constituency elections.

Answers on p. 124

The advantages and disadvantages of electoral systems

The arguments concerning the retention or replacement of first-past-the-post can be summarised as follows.

Arguments for **retention** include these:

- It is a tried and tested system with widespread public support. Voters rejected an alternative system decisively in a 2011 referendum.
- It retains a strong MP–constituency link. This is important for the redress of grievances, an ancient role of MPs.
- It does normally tend to produce strong governments with a working majority in the House of Commons, though this is questionable in view of the results of elections in 2010, 2015 and 2017.
- Replacing it will exchange the known for the unknown, with unquantifiable consequences. There is a fear that the kind of unstable governments which can be found in many parts of the democratic world would be imported into the UK.

Arguments for **replacement** include these:

- The 2010, 2015 and 2017 elections suggest it no longer guarantees a strong, decisive government. This takes away its most potent virtue.
- It produces a very unrepresentative outcome. This is not fair to voters or to the smaller parties.
- Proportional representation means that voters are better served because every vote counts and there are fewer wasted votes.
- Replacement would eliminate the problem of too many safe seats. Safe seats result in too many wasted votes and disillusionment among voters.

> **Exam tip**
>
> Make sure you can quote plenty of statistics from recent elections, both general and devolved, in order to illustrate the impacts of various electoral systems and to be able to compare them.

Tables 3.1–3.4 offer assessments of each of the electoral systems used in the UK.

Table 3.1 An assessment of first-past-the-post

Advantages	Disadvantages
It is easy to understand and produces a clear result in each constituency. The result is also known very quickly.	The overall outcome is not proportional or fair. Some parties win more seats than their support warrants while others win fewer than they deserve.
It produces one single representative for each constituency and so creates a close constituency–MP bond.	It means that many votes are effectively wasted because they can have no impact on the outcome in safe seats. Many seats become part of party 'heartlands' where there is no possibility of a realistic challenge from other parties. It also produces 'electoral deserts' where there is effectively no party competition.
Accountability of the individual MP is clear to the electors.	Votes are of unequal value in that votes in safe seats are less valuable than votes in marginal seats. UKIP votes were of hugely less value than Conservative votes.
Until 2010 the system tended to produce strong governments with a decisive majority in Parliament. However, this has changed in recent years.	It encourages **tactical voting** among some voters and so they abandon the party they really want to support.
It helps to prevent small parties breaking into the system. This is useful if the small parties are undesirable 'extremists'.	It prevents new parties breaking into the system and so produces political 'inertia'.
Arguably the system has stood the test of time. Abandoning it would be a dangerous step into the unknown.	It has, since 1945, always resulted in the winning party securing much less than half the popular vote. In 2015 the winning Conservative Party was elected with just 36.9% of the popular vote — 63.1% of the voters voted against the governing party. In 2005 Labour won the election with a majority of 66 from only 35.2% of the popular vote. This calls into question the legitimacy of the government.
	The system always used to deliver governments with a majority of the seats in the House of Commons. In 2010 it failed to do this. In 2015 the Conservative Party secured only a fragile 12-seat majority and in 2017 it failed to win a majority altogether. It could be argued that if the system fails to deliver a decisive result, it cannot be defended in the future.

Tactical voting When a voter feels they cannot influence the outcome of a constituency election because it is a safe seat or because they support a small party with no hope of winning, they may abandon their first choice and instead vote for their second choice in the hope of influencing the outcome.

Now test yourself

TESTED

5 Look again at recent general elections. Describe an example of each outcome described in the table.

Description	Example
A party won many more seats than its proportion of the popular vote warranted.	
A party won only one seat but won a considerable proportion of the popular vote.	
A party whose representation at Westminster was all but wiped out.	
A party won a parliamentary majority by winning only about one third of the popular vote.	

Answers on p. 124

Table 3.2 An assessment of the additional member system

Advantages	Drawbacks
It produces a broadly proportional outcome and so is fair to all parties.	It produces two classes of representative — those with a constituency and those elected through the lists. The latter tend to be senior.
It gives voters two votes and so more choice.	It is more complex than first-past-the-post. Having two votes can confuse some voters.
It combines preserving constituency representation with a proportional outcome.	It can result in the election of extremist candidates.
	It is more likely to result in **minority** or **coalition** government (see page 46).

Table 3.3 An assessment of the single transferable vote system

Advantages	Drawbacks
It produces a broadly proportional outcome.	It is quite a complex system that some voters do not understand.
It gives voters a wide choice of candidates. Their second and subsequent choices are taken into consideration in the counting.	The vote counting is complicated and can take a long time.
Voters can vote for candidates from different parties and show a preference between candidates of the same party.	It can help candidates with extremist views to be elected.
As there are six representatives per constituency, each voter has a choice of those to represent them and usually can be represented by someone from the party they support.	With six representatives per constituency, the lines of accountability are not clear.
	It is more likely to result in **minority** or **coalition** government.

Table 3.4 An assessment of the supplementary vote system

Advantages	Drawbacks
The winning candidate can claim to have an overall majority of support.	A winning candidate may not enjoy the first-choice support of an overall majority.
It is relatively simple for voters to understand.	The winning candidate may win on second choices.
Voters' first and second choices are relevant.	

Typical mistake

Many students think that proportional representation is an electoral system. It is not. Proportional representation is a description applied to a number of systems which have proportional outcomes, such as STV and list systems.

First-past-the-post compared with other systems

REVISED

Table 3.5 shows first–past–the–post compared with alternative systems on the basis of various objectives.

Table 3.5 Comparing electoral systems on the basis of objectives

Objective	Most appropriate system
Strong, stable government	First-past-the-post
Maximum voter choice	Single transferable vote
A multi-party system	Single transferable vote
Strong constituency representation	First-past-the-post
A proportional outcome	Additional member system
An absolute majority for the winner	Supplementary vote
Votes are of equal value	Single transferable vote

Exam tip

When considering whether the UK should reform the electoral system, divide your answer into two main sections. The first should discuss the impact on the party system and the formation of governments, while the second should discuss the impact on voters and on democracy in general.

How referendums have been used in the UK

REVISED

You should know the details of several referendums to illustrate your answers. Table 3.6 outlines such details.

Table 3.6 Important referendums in the UK since 1997

Year	Issue	Level	Why held	Yes (%)	No (%)	Turnout (%)
1997	Should additional powers be devolved to Scotland and a Scottish Parliament be established?	Scotland	A fundamental change in the system of government needed popular consent.	74.3	25.7	60.4
1997	Should additional powers be devolved to Wales and a Welsh Assembly be established?	Wales	A fundamental change in the system of government needed popular consent.	50.3	49.7	50.1

➡

Exam practice answers and quick quizzes at **www.hoddereducation.co.uk/myrevisionnotesdownloads**

Year	Issue	Level	Why held	Yes (%)	No (%)	Turnout (%)
1998	Should the Belfast Agreement be implemented?	Northern Ireland	This required support across the whole divided community.	71.7	28.9	81.0
2004	Should additional powers be devolved to northeast England and a regional assembly established?	Northeast England	A fundamental change in the system of government needed popular consent.	22.1	77.9	47.7
2011	Should the UK adopt the alternative vote system for general elections?	National	The coalition government was divided on the issue of electoral reform.	32.1	67.9	42.2
2014	Should Scotland become a completely independent country?	Scotland	A fundamental question about who governs Scotland.	44.7	55.3	84.6
2016	Should the UK remain a member of the EU?	National	A fundamental constitutional question. The governing Conservative Party was split on the issue and seeking to meet the challenge of UKIP.	48.1	51.9	72.2

The reasons why referendums have been held in the UK include the following:

● An issue might be divisive within government and/or within the nation, so a referendum can settle the issue and unite the population. Example: the referendum on EU membership, 2016.
● An issue may be of huge constitutional significance and so require the direct consent of the people. Example: the 2014 referendum on Scottish independence.
● It helps to entrench and safeguard constitutional changes. This may be necessary when the community requires reassurance that the change is permanent. Example: the referendum on the Belfast Agreement in Northern Ireland, 1998.
● To judge public opinion on an issue, especially where a change in taxation may be involved. Example: local referendums on congestion charges.

> **Typical mistake**
>
> Although it is governments and Parliament that decide when referendums will be held in the UK and what the wording will be, it would be a mistake to believe that they may manipulate the outcome. The conduct of referendum campaigns is strongly regulated by the politically neutral Electoral Commission.

The impact of referendums in the UK

REVISED

It can be argued that some referendums are successful and others create problems. Some also have mixed consequences. The context of a number of key referendums is shown here.

Successful exercises:
● The referendum on Scottish independence did seem to have settled the issue. There was a high turnout and a decisive result.

- The local referendums on the introduction of congestion charges in cities successfully established that public opinion was against the idea.
- Votes on Scottish devolution in 1997 and on a new settlement in Northern Ireland in 1998 were decisive and led to widespread consent to the changes.

Unsuccessful exercises:

- The referendum on Welsh devolution in 1997 produced a narrow majority on a low turnout. This led to confusion over how much devolution Wales should be granted.
- The 2011 referendum on electoral reform produced a decisive result though on a low turnout. It is argued that the 'No' vote was more an expression of opposition to the Liberal Democrats than it was related to the issue.

> **Exam tip**
>
> When discussing and analysing the use of referendums, make sure you can quote statistical and political examples from recent referendums to illustrate your answer and to provide evidence.

The case for and against referendums

REVISED

The case for and against the continued use of referendums is a balanced one. The main issues include those shown in Table 3.7.

Table 3.7 An assessment of the use of referendums

Arguments for	Arguments against
Referendums are the purest form of democracy, uncorrupted by the filter of representative democracy. They demonstrate the pure will of the people, as shown in the EU vote. They are a direct expression of popular consent.	The issue may be too complex for people to understand. The electoral system, which was the subject of the 2011 referendum, was difficult to understand. The issue of EU membership was also a difficult one.
Referendums can help to unite a divided society, as occurred with the decisive result of the 1998 vote on the Belfast Agreement.	Referendums can cause social rifts. They are designed to heal divisions but can sometimes cause them. This arguably occurred both in 2014 in Scotland and in 2016 in the EU referendum.
Referendums can solve conflicts *within* the government and the rest of the political system and so stave off a crisis. This was especially the case with the EU referendums in both 1975 and 2016.	There is a danger that the excessive use of referendums may undermine the authority of representative democracy. This has been a particular danger in some states in the USA.
Referendums are particularly useful when the *expressed* (as opposed to *implied*) consent of the people is important, so that the decision will be respected. This was very true of the votes on devolution in 1997.	A referendum can represent the 'tyranny of the majority'. This means that the majority that wins the vote can use their victory to force the minority to accept a change that is against their interests. The Scots, Northern Irish and Londoners, who voted strongly to stay in the EU in 2016, claimed they were being tyrannised by the English majority.
A recent argument is that people are better informed in modern times and so are in a better position to make crucial decisions.	Voters may be swayed by emotional rather than rational appeals. It may also be that they are influenced by false information. This may have occurred during the EU referendum.
	Some questions should not be reduced to a simple Yes/No answer; they are more complicated. Certainly the 2011 question on electoral reform is an example of this. Perhaps several *different* options should have been considered, not just one.

Debates on electoral systems

REVISED

Elections and first-past-the-post

An assessment of elections and first-past-the-post in the UK looks like this.

Positive features

- There is relatively little corruption. Some electoral fraud takes place in some areas but it is rare and usually detected. The secrecy of the ballot is virtually guaranteed. The counting of votes is carefully and thoroughly regulated. The conduct of elections is safeguarded by the Electoral Commission, which is independent of government.
- The constituency system ensures clear representation for citizens.
- Before 2010 general elections tended to produce governments with a decisive majority. This tendency may well return in the future — 2010–17 may have been rare exceptions.
- UK elections are free in that it is relatively easy and cheap for any citizen to stand for election and virtually all adults are permitted to vote.

Negative features

- The first-past-the-post system used for general and local elections in England and Wales is widely acknowledged to be unfair and certainly unrepresentative. Many votes are wasted and votes are of unequal value.
- Small parties find it difficult to gain a foothold because of the electoral system in England.
- UK general elections produce governments that do not enjoy a majority of the support of the electorate. In recent elections, the winning party has failed to achieve 40% of the popular vote.

Proportional representation

An assessment of proportional representation as used in the UK looks like this.

Positive features

- Proportional systems produce a more accurate reflection of public support for various parties.
- Small parties receive a fairer degree of representation and are given the chance to establish themselves.
- There are fewer wasted votes, which will improve public engagement with electoral politics.
- There is less need for voters to vote tactically.
- In systems such as STV and AMS, voters have more choice.
- In pure proportional systems, every vote counts.

Negative features

- Some systems, notably STV, are more difficult to understand.
- Proportional systems increase the danger of small, extremist parties gaining a hold.

- It is much more likely that no party will gain an overall majority in the legislature. This creates the possibility of weak, unstable governments, either coalitions or minority governments.
- In coalitions and other governing agreements, small parties gain a disproportionate amount of influence, well beyond the degree of support they enjoy.

Electoral systems and types of government

REVISED

Various electoral systems tend to produce particular forms of government — see Table 3.8.

Table 3.8 Electoral systems and forms of government

Electoral system	Typical form of government resulting	Example
First-past-the-post	Single-party majority government	UK
STV	Power sharing among several parties	Northern Ireland
Additional member system	Two-party coalition government or one-party **minority government**	Scotland
List system	**Coalition government**	Much of Europe

There are exceptions to these tendencies:
- 2010–15 coalition government in the UK.
- 2012–16 single-party government in Scotland.

> **Coalition government**
> Where a government is formed from more than one party. In a coalition, seats in the government are shared among more than one party and proposals have to be agreed in advance by all members of the coalition.
>
> **Minority government** A government that does not command a parliamentary majority. Such governments are unstable and have difficulty surviving. They have to seek a consensus of support for all their proposals.

Revision activity

Make sure you thoroughly revise the following:
1 An example of an election that produced a coalition government and why this happened.
2 An example of an election that produced a very large majority for one party and why this happened.
3 An example of an election to a devolved assembly that produced a minority government and why this happened.

Impact of electoral systems on party representation

REVISED

Various electoral systems tend to produce different party systems — see Table 3.9.

Table 3.9 Electoral systems and party systems

Electoral system	Typical form of party system	Example
First-past-the-post	Two-party system	UK
STV	Multi-party system	Northern Ireland
Additional member system	Four-party system	Scotland
List system	Multi-party system	Much of Europe

Revision activity

Revise the following key facts:
1 The kind of party system that exists in Scotland and why.
2 The kind of party system that exists in Wales and why.
3 The kind of party system that exists in Northern Ireland and why.

There are exceptions to these tendencies:

- 1997–2015 Small parties did make progress in the UK.
- 2012–17 Scotland had a single dominant party.

Impact of electoral systems on voter choice

REVISED

Various electoral systems tend to produce different impacts for voters — see Table 3.10.

Table 3.10 Electoral systems and voter choice

Electoral system	Effect on voter choice	Example
First-past-the-post	Little choice for voters. Votes are of unequal value. Many wasted votes.	UK
STV	Wide voter choice. Few wasted votes. More diverse group of candidates.	Northern Ireland
Additional member system	Voters have two votes. Voters may split the votes between two parties. Fewer wasted votes.	Scotland
List system	No wasted votes. Votes are of equal value.	Much of Europe

Typical mistake

When considering multi-party systems in the UK, many students forget to consider the devolved assemblies. First-past-the-post may produce a two-party system in general elections, but proportional systems have a different outcome in Scotland, Wales and Northern Ireland.

Exam practice

AS

1 Describe the main features of a referendum. [10]
2 Describe the main functions of elections. [10]
3 Using the source, explain the main consequences of the introduction of proportional representation. [10]

There are many arguments for introducing a proportional electoral system for UK general elections. Most of them revolve around the unfairness of the current system, in particular in relation to small parties being able to gain a reasonable amount of representation. It is not surprising, therefore, that the calls are mostly coming from those parties. However, the picture is, in reality, more complex.

PR will take away the tendency of first-past-the-post to produce a two-party system and to distort the relationship between votes cast and seats won by each party. Every vote will count and the outcome of elections will reflect more accurately what the voters want. There will be fewer wasted votes and this ought to create more confidence in the system. It is often argued that one of the reasons for falling turnout figures in recent decades is that too many people feel their voices are unheard. Certainly, the supporters of such parties as UKIP, the Greens and the Liberal Democrats would echo this argument.

One of the main culprits is the prevalence of safe seats. Possibly as many as half the parliamentary seats are considered to be safe. This means that the outcome seems inevitable and the seat rarely changes hands. Voters in safe seats feel their vote is useless whether they support the winning party or one of the other parties. The only way to beat the system, some argue, is to vote tactically. But tactical voting seems to be a denial of democracy. Why should people feel they cannot support their first-choice party? The introduction of PR would certainly take away the need for tactical voting.

Source: original material

In your response you must use knowledge and understanding to analyse points that are only in the source. You will **not** be rewarded for introducing any additional points that are not in the source.

4 'Referendums are not as democratic as might seem the case at first sight.' How far do you agree with this view? [30]

A-level

1 Evaluate the extent to which the first-past-the-post electoral system promotes strong and stable government. [30]
2 Evaluate the extent to which proportional representation promotes a democratic multi-party system. [30]
3 Using the source, evaluate the extent to which it is now essential that the UK introduces a proportional system for general elections. [30]

There are a number of features of recent general elections that point to the need for a different electoral system for the UK. The 2015 general election was a case in point. UKIP won nearly 4 million votes and yet this translated into just one seat. In Scotland, conversely, the Scottish National Party won 50% of the popular vote and yet won 56 out of the 59 seats available. When we add to that the fact that the Conservative government won only 36.9% of the popular vote in the UK but was rewarded with a 12-seat majority, we must seriously question the way the system works.

This kind of bias has, of course, been known for many years, so why the urgency for a decision today? There are a number of reasons, but the outcome of the three elections in 2010, 2015 and 2017 gave the argument fresh impetus. In 2010, the system produced a hung parliament, in 2015 the Conservatives only just scraped home with a majority of 12 seats, and then came 2017. In the 2017 general election campaign, prime minister May placed great emphasis on the need for 'strong and stable' government. She was referring to the negotiations for the UK's exit from the EU, but she could have been referring to the debate about the electoral system. First-past-the-post used to produce such governments and it was fully expected that it would do so again.

The result was a huge surprise. Once again first-past-the-post failed in its first function — that of producing a majority government. With three consecutive indecisive results behind them, even Conservatives began to lose faith in the electoral system.

Liberals, meanwhile, look to the interests of individual voters. Wasted votes and votes of unequal value are a matter of increasing concern. With proportional representation, votes are rarely wasted and most votes count. Depending on which system is introduced, it could also be that voters would have more choice.

Source: original material

In your response you must:
● compare the different opinions in the source
● consider this view and the alternative to this view in a balanced way
● use knowledge and understanding to help you analyse and evaluate.

Answers and quick quiz 3 online

ONLINE

Summary

You should now have an understanding of:
● the workings of first-past-the-post
● the workings of the additional member system
● the workings of the single transferable vote system
● the workings of the supplementary vote system
● the impact of all the electoral systems described above
● several recent referendums used in the UK
● the use of referendums to determine key constitutional and political issues
● the arguments for and against the introduction of proportional representation for general elections
● how voters would be advantaged by proportional representation
● how the formation of governments and the party system would be affected by different electoral systems.

4 Voting behaviour and the media

When revising general elections to use as case studies, you should consider the following features and master them:

- What were the main features of the outcome? How did each party perform?
- What were the main changes since the previous election? Which parties gained ground, which lost ground?
- What were the main issues at the election?
- What were the main factors that influenced the outcome? Was it valence issues, leadership factors, economic factors, long-term changes in social factors?
- How was the political system affected by the outcome? Did government change? What was the size of the government majority? Was there a hung parliament?

The 1979 general election

REVISED

Main features of the outcome

- Labour's representation went down by 62 and the Conservatives' up by 50.
- The Conservative majority was 43.
- No small parties won a significant number of seats.
- The Scottish National Party lost 9 of their 11 seats in Scotland, reflecting a loss of interest in devolution at that time.

Main changes since the last election

- The UK moved from a Labour government with no majority to a Conservative government with a comfortable majority.
- The first female prime minister was elected.

Main issues

- There had been a wave of public-sector strikes in 1978–79. People punished Labour for not controlling trade union power.
- The economy was in a poor state, in particular concerning inflation, though this had been falling. Labour became associated with high inflation.
- The extent to which the state should regulate and control industry as opposed to the operation of free markets was an issue.

Main influences on the outcome

- Labour ran a poor election campaign, implying that the country should not elect a woman.
- Labour was not trusted on the economy.
- Labour was beginning to appear disunited between its left wing and its moderates.
- The Conservative promise to expand home ownership was popular.
- The growing size of the middle class and shrinking working class gave the Conservatives a natural advantage.

How was government affected by the outcome?

- The UK moved from a period of indecisive, weak government with a tiny majority to government with a working majority.
- It marked the beginning of 18 consecutive years of Conservative government.
- The bulk of the electorate moved towards a centrist or right-wing attitude to most issues.

The 1997 general election

REVISED

Main features of the outcome

- It was a landslide victory for the Labour Party under Blair.
- The Liberal Democrats made a breakthrough, winning 46 seats at Westminster.
- The effects of the electoral system exaggerated the scale of Labour's victory — 43% of the vote was converted into 63% of the seats.

Main changes since the last election

- The Conservatives lost a total of 178 seats, Labour gained 145.
- The Liberal Democrats gained 28 seats.
- The Labour vote had risen by 8.8% since 1987, while the Conservative vote had fallen by 11.2%.

Main issues

- The 1990s had seen an economic recession for which the Conservatives were blamed.
- The National Health Service was considered to be in decline.
- Education funding and standards were falling.
- Crime was at high levels.

Main influences on the outcome

- Blair was seen as a charismatic, dynamic leader while John Major, the Conservative prime minister, was viewed as dull and uninspiring.
- Blair, with his 'third way' policies, was able to appeal to the growing middle class. He succeeded in shedding his party's reputation for being too socialist and reckless with public finances.
- The electorate was weary of many years of Conservative rule and wanted a change.
- The media showed strong support for Labour.

How was government affected by the outcome?

- The election marked the beginning of 13 years of Labour rule, during which the party won three general elections.
- Labour won a huge parliamentary majority which made it possible for it to commence a significant programme of social, economic and constitutional reform.
- The beginnings of a three-party system can be seen at this election.

The 2010 general election

Main features of the outcome

- There was a dramatic outcome — the first hung parliament since February 1974.
- The Conservative Party won 36.1% of the popular vote. Along with the Liberal Democrats' 23%, the coalition government held 59.1% of popular support.
- The Liberal Democrats continued their resurgence by winning 23% of the popular vote and 57 seats.

Main changes since the last election

- More than with previous elections, this was a leadership election.
- It was clear that the electorate had become more volatile than before.
- Opinion polls, largely accurate in the past, proved to be inaccurate this time, partly because of increased voter volatility.
- Turnout, which had slumped to below 60% in 2005, recovered somewhat to 65% in 2010.

Main issues

- This was almost a 'one-issue' election. The state of the economy in the face of the major financial crisis engulfing the capitalist world at the time was the overwhelming concern.
- The Labour Party was blamed for the state of the UK financial system.
- The alarming growth in government debt brought back memories of Labour as a 'tax-and-spend party'.
- A key issue was whether the UK should spend its way out of the crisis or institute a programme of austerity (higher taxes and lower government spending) to deal with it.

Main influences on the outcome

- Leadership was a key issue. Prime minister Gordon Brown was regarded as weak and indecisive as well as dull and lacking charisma. David Cameron presented a fresher, more decisive image.
- During the campaign the spectre of a coalition between Labour and the Scottish National Party was raised in the media, as a hung parliament was expected. This proved to be an unpopular prospect for many voters, so they switched to the Conservatives.
- The opinion polls, which pointed to a hung parliament, had an influence as they may have changed some voters' minds about which party to support.
- There was a relentless press campaign criticising Brown as a leader.

How was government affected by the outcome?

- Labour failed to form a coalition with the Liberal Democrats or the SNP, so the Conservatives were invited to join with the Liberal Democrats.
- There followed five years of problematic, fragile coalition government.
- The UK seemed to be moving further towards a three-party system.

The 2017 general election

Main features of the outcome

- This was an extraordinary election in many ways. Early forecasts of a Conservative landslide were dispelled in the last two weeks of the campaign.
- It produced a hung parliament, with the Conservatives the largest party but short of an overall majority.
- The Conservative Party gained an increased share of the vote but lost seats, while Labour's share of the vote rose nearly 10% and they gained seats.
- The expected Liberal Democrat revival did not happen. UKIP lost most of its share of the vote and its one seat. The Greens faltered and the SNP lost seats in Scotland.
- The reputation of Labour leader Jeremy Corbyn was enormously enhanced, while that of Theresa May was damaged.
- In order to govern, the Conservatives had to reach a **confidence and supply** agreement with the Democratic Unionist Party of Northern Ireland (with ten seats) to give them an overall majority. A large grant of £1 billion was awarded to the province in return for DUP support.

> **Confidence and supply**
> Confidence refers to the ability of the government to retain the confidence of the majority of MPs, tested occasionally in a vote of no confidence. Supply refers to the ability of the government to have its financial plans (budget) approved by the House of Commons each year.

Main changes since the last election

- UKIP ceased to be a force in UK politics.
- The SNP lost its dominance in Scotland and the issue of Scottish independence was put on the 'back burner'.
- The Conservatives, having enjoyed a 12-seat majority after 2015, became a minority government but increased their share of the vote by 5.5%.
- Labour increased its share of the vote by 9.6%.

Main issues

- There was a clear choice between the left-wing policies of Labour and the centrist, moderate policies of the Conservative Party. This was the clearest choice to be presented since the ideology-driven election of 1983.
- The Conservatives campaigned on the issue of strong leadership, the ability to conclude Brexit negotiations successfully and 'strong and stable' government.
- Labour campaigned on such radical policies as nationalisation of the railways, Royal Mail and water companies, rises in taxation on the wealthy, large increases in expenditure on health and education, abolition of university tuition fees and free nursery care.

Main influences on the outcome

- Jeremy Corbyn enjoyed a successful campaign and raised his profile and personal support, while Theresa May suffered a poor campaign and her reputation was damaged.
- The young voted in much larger numbers than in the recent past, giving a significant boost to the Labour Party.
- Many former UKIP voters gave their support to one of the two main parties, resulting in two-party dominance. UKIP had a poor campaign. Similarly, 21 former SNP seats in Scotland were won by Labour or the Conservatives.

- The bulk of the press was pro-Conservative but the Labour Party, using social media extensively, was able to thwart the opposition of the traditional press.

Exam tip

You need to quote evidence from at least three recent elections when analysing voting behaviour.

How was government affected by the outcome?

- A hung parliament resulted.
- A minority Conservative government took over, supported by the ten MPs from the DUP to give it a majority on key votes.

Now test yourself

TESTED

1 Look at the following descriptions. In each case identify which general election conforms to the description:
  - The opinion polls predicted a hung parliament but one party won outright with a narrow majority.
  - Voting for the Liberal Democrats collapsed and they lost most of their seats.
  - The sitting prime minister had a poor media image, which contributed to his party losing power after many years in office.
  - The *Sun* newspaper claimed, in a headline, that it had won the election for the Conservatives.

Answers on p. 124

Party manifestos and election campaigns

REVISED

The key factors in election campaigns which may affect the outcome of a general election include the following:
- **The manifestos (on which a party's mandate is based).** In 2017 the publication of the manifestos led to a narrowing of the gap in opinion polls between Labour and the Conservatives. However, normally manifestos make little impact.
- **Leadership debates on TV.** In 2010 the impressive performance of Liberal Democrat leader Nick Clegg and the weak showing of Labour prime minister Gordon Brown were influential on their parties' fortunes. In 2015 David Cameron outperformed Labour leader Ed Miliband.
- **The press can be influential if it shows a distinct bias towards one side.** This may have contributed to Labour's loss in 2015. The press can also influence through its image of the party leaders.
- **Issues can be favourable or unfavourable to the parties.** Each party tends to concentrate on the issues on which it feels itself to be strong during the campaign. Thus they tend to cancel each other out. Evidence suggests issues reinforce existing voting intentions rather than changing them.

Manifesto A set of commitments produced by each party at the start of an election campaign.

Mandate The authority, granted by the people at elections, to a party which will form the government. The newly elected government has the authority to carry out its election proposals.

Typical mistake

Do not place too much emphasis on the influence of party manifestos on election outcomes. Most voters do not read manifestos.

Typical mistake

Do not assume that the outcome of elections depends solely on the performance and image of the governing party. The image of the opposition is of almost equal importance.

Class and voting

The story of social class and voting is one of steady decline in its influence. Table 4.1 demonstrates this.

Table 4.1 Class AB voting for the Conservatives

Election year	% class AB voting Conservative	% class DE voting Labour
1964	78	64
1987	57	53
1997	59	59
2010	40	40
2015	45	41
2017	43	59

Source: Ipsos MORI

Typical mistake

Do not confuse class with income levels. Class is about background and lifestyle and may not coincide with income levels.

Factors other than class affecting voting — demographic factors

Age

There are other factors besides class that affect voting, such as age, as illustrated in Table 4.2.

Table 4.2 Age and voting in four general elections

Age range	1979			1997			2010			2017		
	% Con	% Lab	% All*	% Con	% Lab	% LD*	% Con	% Lab	% LD*	% Con	% Lab	% LD*
18–24	42	41	12	27	49	16	30	31	30	18	67	7
25–34	43	38	15	28	49	16	30	29	29	22	58	8
35–44**	46	35	16	28	48	17	31	26	26	30	50	8
45–54				31	41	20	28	26	26	40	39	8
55–64***	47	38	13	36	39	17	28	23	23	47	33	8
65+				36	41	17	44	31	16	59	23	10
Total all ages	45	38	14	31	43	17	36	29	23	42	40	8

* The third party was the SDP/Liberal Alliance in 1979, the Liberal Democrats thereafter.

** The 1979 figures are for 35–54.

*** The 1979 figures are for 55+.

Source: Ipsos MORI; Ashcroft Polling (for 2017)

The conclusions we can reach from these data about age and voting are as follows:

- The 18–24 age group is much more likely to support the Labour Party than the Conservatives.
- The 35–44 age group is the most likely range to support the Liberal Democrats.
- The older a voter is, the more likely they are to support the Conservative Party.

It is also true that the younger a voter is, the more likely they are to support two of the UK's most radical parties, the Greens and the Scottish National Party.

Gender

Gender has little or no impact on voting intentions. Women and men display remarkably similar political attitudes.

Ethnicity

Ethnicity is a major predictor of how a person will vote — see Table 4.3.

Table 4.3 Ethnicity and voting

Election	% BME voting Conservative	% BME voting Labour	% BME voting Liberal Democrat
1997	18	70	9
2010	16	60	20
2015	23	65	4
2017	21	65	6

BME = black and minority ethnic   Source: Ipsos MORI

Region

- The south of England is heavily dominated by the Conservative Party.
- The same is true of the Midlands, though to a slightly lesser extent.
- The north of England is Labour dominated.
- Outside London and Scotland, UKIP support is evenly spread.
- Scotland is heavily dominated by the SNP.
- London is different from the rest of the south of England in that Labour has more support in the city.

Table 4.4 shows how the regions voted in the 2017 general election.

Table 4.4 2017 general election, voting by region

Region	% Conservative	% Labour	% Liberal Democrat	% SNP or Plaid Cymru
North of England	37.2	52.9	5.0	n/a
South of England	45.7	25.5	9.9	n/a
Midlands	49.7	41.6	4.4	n/a
London	34.9	43.7	7.7	n/a
Scotland	14.9	24.3	7.5	36.9
Wales	27.2	36.9	6.5	10.4

Table 4.5 summarises the influence of various factors on voting behaviour.

Table 4.5 The influence of social and democratic factors

Factor	Estimated influence
Gender	There is virtually no difference in voting habits between men and women, though there is a slight tendency for women to favour Labour.
Age	This is a key factor. Older voters favour the Conservatives (and UKIP) very significantly. Young voters have a Labour bias and also tend to support the Green Party.
Ethnicity	This is also significant, although there are signs that it is weakening as a factor. A further trend is for more established immigrant groups to move towards favouring the Conservative Party.
Class	Class used to be the most important determinant of voting behaviour but is becoming much less influential. It remains significant, however.
Region	There are wide regional variations in voting patterns. Scotland is the most remarkable currently, with the SNP enjoying complete dominance. The south of England is solidly Conservative, leaving Labour with a mountain to climb in that region. UKIP made inroads into Labour's former dominance of northern England. This leads to what are known as electoral heartlands, where only one party wins any seats.

Revision activity

Make sure you know the characteristics of voting in these regions:
1 Southwest England.
2 Northeast England.
3 Northern Ireland.
4 Wales.

Now test yourself

TESTED

2 Answer the following questions about the voting behaviour of different demographic groups:
● Which demographic group is mostly likely to vote for the Green Party?
● Which age group is heavily biased towards voting Conservative?
● Which social class is most likely to vote UKIP?
● Which demographic group used to be more likely to vote Labour but now is more likely to vote Conservative?
● Which age group has the lowest election turnout figures?

Answers on p. 124

Analysis of voting behaviour

REVISED

You should have a good grasp of the following short-term influences on voting behaviour.

Partisanship and voting attachment

- **Class dealignment** has occurred. This means that the old strong links between the working class and Labour and the middle class and the Conservatives have weakened. As a result of class dealignment, people display weaker party attachments: that is, they demonstrate **partisan dealignment**.
- The parties had tended to adopt centrist policies which could attract a wider range of voter support. Labour in 2017, however, adopted a radical left-wing programme in order to try to re-engage its traditional supporters.
- There is growing support for smaller parties such as UKIP, the Green Party and the Scottish Nationalists.
- There is a general widespread dissatisfaction with the performance of parties at Westminster (demonstrated by UKIP voting in 2015 and low turnouts), so people feel less attachment to them.
- Party membership has fallen dramatically (with some recovery in Labour membership in 2016), so there are many fewer committed party supporters.

Class dealignment A tendency, increasing in modern times, for people to disassociate themselves from one particular class and its dominant political attitudes.

Partisan dealignment People who, in the past, identified themselves closely with one particular party are increasingly seeing themselves as independent of any such attachment.

Valence

Valence is one of the key factors in voting behaviour. It stands in opposition to **positional voting** where voters are looking at specific policies or groups of policies when making decisions about whom to vote for. Valence refers to the following attitudes towards the parties at elections:

- **Governing competency**. Does the party appear to be decisive? Did it govern well when it was last in power? It refers to such qualities as strength, decisiveness and sensitivity to public opinion. This was a problem for Labour in 2010 and the Liberal Democrats in 2015.
- **Economic competence.** How well did the party manage the economy last time it was in power? Do its current leaders and their policies inspire trust and suggest reliability? Labour lost confidence on economic management after the financial crash of 2008. The Conservatives developed a positive reputation on such competence, which helped them in 2017.

Valence A belief among voters that a party is competent and is well led. It is said by some commentators to be the key factor in voting behaviour. Valence ignores specific policies and refers instead to the image of the party in voters' minds.

Governing competency A general feeling among voters that a party is either very competent in governing or much less competent. Competency refers largely to sound economic policies, sensible foreign policy and decisiveness in office.

- **How united is the party?** Voters trust united parties but not disunited ones. The Conservatives lost elections in 2001 and 2005 partly because the party was divided within itself. It was a serious problem for Labour in 2017 also.
- **Are the leaders admired and trusted?** The Liberal Democrats did well in 2010 because leader Nick Clegg was liked and respected. Nevertheless, he lost respect after that and was heavily defeated in 2015. Ed Miliband, Labour's leader from 2010 to 2015, was not well respected and was a major cause of the party's defeat in 2015. In 2017, Theresa May was more trusted and respected than Jeremy Corbyn, the Labour leader, although Corbyn recovered some ground during the election campaign.

Rational choice

This concerns the identification of 'salient' or very important issues at stake in the election. Many voters are influenced by such salient issues, so parties often make them the main elements in their election campaigns.

Salient issues in *all* general elections in the UK include:
- the state of the economy
- the state of the National Health Service
- the state of education
- immigration issues
- trends in crime and law and order.

In addition, in the 2017 general election the salient issues were:
- how the UK was going to exit the EU and what kind of deal could be done with the EU
- the problems in how to fund social care of the elderly
- the future of the UK's nuclear capability
- how much regulation or public ownership there should be of 'big business'
- how the tax burden should be distributed between high-, middle- and low-income groups
- how much protection there should be for workers against poor employment practices
- the extent to which the government should 'spend and borrow' its way towards economic growth as opposed to concentrating on financial responsibility and the reduction of public-sector debt.

Issue voting

Issue voting is similar to rational choice, but here voters are concentrating on one single issue or a group of related issues. Voters' choice is often divided into two types:
- **Instrumental voting.** This is what the voter thinks will be best *in their own interests* — for example, which party will reduce my taxes? Which party will pay me most benefits? Which party is most likely to give me job security?
- **Expressive voting.** When a voter thinks not of themselves but of the good of the whole community — for example, which party has the best environmental policies or law and order position or foreign policy?

Both are rational because they compare the pros and cons of supporting a particular party. Issue voting may be influenced by the contents of **party manifestos** (see page 53), though few voters read them thoroughly.

Turnout

The level of turnout can influence the outcome of an election. This is because different demographic groups usually demonstrate different turnout levels. This is usually to the advantage of the Conservative Party. The young, who tend to be more left wing, vote in much smaller numbers than over-65s, who are more likely to be Conservatives. The same is true of low-income groups, who mostly support Labour but vote in smaller numbers. Higher-income groups turn out in larger numbers and tend to be Conservative. The main reason for low turnout are **disillusion** and **apathy**, which are more prominent among the young.

> **Disillusion and apathy** Traits that force down levels of turnout. They may be the result of low esteem for the political class or a general lack of interest in politics and a suspicion that politics cannot change things for many people.

Exam tip

You need to be able to discuss the reasons why people do not vote and which people do not vote, almost as much as why they do vote.

Party leaders and voting behaviour

The quality of the party leaders is an issue which stands alone in voting behaviour. The typical qualities that voters like to support are listed below. In each case a good example of the reputation of a leader is shown:

- Record in office (Margaret Thatcher 1979–87).
- Compassion (John Major 1990–92, Jeremy Corbyn 2017).
- Decisiveness (Tony Blair 1997–2001).
- Strong leadership (Margaret Thatcher, Theresa May 2017).
- Clear vision (Tony Blair, Nicola Sturgeon for the SNP).
- Communication skills (David Cameron 2010–16, Jeremy Corbyn).
- Populist appeal (Nigel Farage 2015).

Table 4.6 summarises the various non-social factors that affect voting behaviour.

Table 4.6 Non-social factors in voting behaviour

Factor type	Description
Valence	The general image of the party — trustworthiness, competence, unity, etc.
Rational choice	Which party has the best policies either for the individual voter or for the community as a whole. This largely concerns salient issues.
Issue voting	Which single issue or group of issues attracts some voters.
Leadership issues	Which leader is perceived to have the best qualities.

Now test yourself

3 Look at the following descriptions. What is being described in each case?

Description	What is being described
A general term for the party image and competence as it affects voting support	
The increasing tendency for people not to consider themselves part of a particular social class or to adopt the typical attitudes associated with that class	
The increasing tendency for people not to consider themselves closely attached to one particular party and its policies	
The name given to the idea that a party that wins an election has the democratic authority to carry out its manifesto commitments	

4 Identify three demographic groups that are most likely to vote for a left-wing party.

Answers on pp. 124–25

The role and impact of the media in elections, bias and persuasion

Table 4.7 shows the political stance of UK newspapers.

Table 4.7 The political affiliations of the main UK newspapers at the 2017 election

Newspaper	Political preference	Circulation (000s)
Sun	Strongly Conservative	1,667
Daily Mail	Strongly Conservative	1,514
Daily Mirror	Strongly Labour	725
Daily Telegraph	Strongly Conservative	472
The Times	Moderately Conservative	451
Daily Star	No preference	443
Daily Express	Strongly UKIP	393
Financial Times	Conservative/Liberal Democrat	189
Guardian	Moderately Labour	157
Independent	Conservative/Liberal Democrat	59

Typical mistake

Do not assume that because most newspapers lean towards the Conservatives this means the Conservatives must always win. Many newspaper readers do not necessarily agree with the political stance of the paper they read.

The key issues concerning press influence include the following:

- Newspapers may contribute to setting the agenda — identifying certain issues which may appear most significant — and so favour some parties more than others. This often applies to the economy.
- Newspapers may influence people concerning the image of leaders. Ed Miliband suffered from a major press campaign in 2015 suggesting he was ineffective.

- The press may influence people's image of the parties in general (valence), which may affect some floating voters.
- Even though newspapers may have little influence over voters, some politicians *believe* they do and so they can be influenced to change their policies to please newspaper proprietors.
- Newspapers in the UK are free, so their bias is inevitable.
- The evidence suggests that newspaper opinion, as expressed in their comment pages, reinforces existing political attitudes but rarely changes them.
- The broadcast media are not permitted to show any political bias, so there is no evidence that they influence political opinion.
- Social media are active in election campaigns but their influence cannot be estimated as so many different opinions are expressed on social media.

> **Exam tip**
>
> It is important to know whom the newspapers supported in the most recent general election as well as how accurate or inaccurate the opinion polls were.

Opinion polls and elections

REVISED

The problems concerning opinion polls include a number of features. The main issues are as follows:

- The media and political parties pay a great deal of attention to opinion polls.
- In recent elections and referendums, opinion polls have proved to be inaccurate. For example, they failed to predict the Conservative general election victory in 2015, the 'Leave' vote in the 2016 EU referendum and a hung parliament in June 2017.
- Voters may adjust their intentions according to what the polls are revealing. For example, some voters may have decided not to vote Labour in 2015 as they feared a Labour–SNP coalition. Some may have voted to leave the EU as a protest, as they expected the outcome to be 'Remain' and their vote would not matter.
- If the polls are showing a clear outcome one way or another, it may discourage people from voting at all.
- Parties may adjust their policies as a result of opinion poll findings, even though those findings may be inaccurate.

> **Revision activity**
>
> Learn the meaning of the following terms related to opinion polls:
> 1 Quota sampling.
> 2 Random sampling.
> 3 Margin of error.

Table 4.8 considers whether the findings of opinion polls should be published before elections.

Table 4.8 Should the publication of opinion polls be banned in the run-up to elections?

For banning them	Against banning them
They may influence the way people vote.	It would infringe the principle of freedom of expression.
They have proved to be inaccurate, so they mislead the public.	If they are banned they will become available privately for organisations that can afford to pay for them.
Arguably politicians should not be slaves to changing public opinion as expressed in the polls.	Polls give valuable information about people's attitudes, which can guide politicians usefully.
	They would still be published abroad and people could access them through the internet.

> **Typical mistake**
>
> Do not assume that opinion polls are always wrong. They do build in to their research a degree of tolerance, usually 3–4% either way, so if they are less than 4% out with their prediction they have been reasonably accurate.

Now test yourself

5 Look at these statements about opinion polls. Which of them do you think might affect the outcome of an election and in what way?

Opinion poll forecast	Likely impact
They forecast a landslide victory for one party.	
They predict a hung parliament.	
They predict a very close result.	
They predict that an extreme right-wing party will do well.	
They predict that an extreme left-wing party will do well.	

Answers on p. 125

Exam practice

AS

1 Describe the influence of social class on voting behaviour. [10]
2 Describe the main impacts of the additional member system. [10]
3 Using the source, explain the significance of region on voting behaviour. [10]

One of the most startling features of the 2015 general election was the fact that the Liberal Democrats lost all of their 15 seats in the Southwest of England. The former dominance of this region by the Liberal Democrats is something of a mystery. It used to be that the party attracted the support of small farmers, who abound in this area, but this group is now more likely to support UKIP or the Conservatives. It may also have been the result of a feeling in the far Southwest that they had long been ignored by the main parties. Certainly, there is little heavy industry in the region, which explains Labour's poor showing, but it was never clear why the Conservatives did not do better. In 2015, however, normal service was resumed.

Normally regional variations in voting can be put down to economic factors. Prosperous regions are much more likely to return Conservative MPs, while working-class districts are bound to be Labour-dominated. Turning to London, the position is less clear. Here the prevalence of ethnic minority voters favours Labour (which is also true in the big cities of the North and the Midlands), while the outer suburbs are solid Conservative country. Then there is Scotland — now completely dominated by the SNP. The collapse of Labour in Scotland after 2005 was perhaps even more dramatic than the Liberal Democrats' loss of the Southwest.

Source: original material

In your response you must use knowledge and understanding to analyse points that are only in the source. You will **not** be rewarded for introducing any additional points that are not in the source.

4 'Voters are less interested in policies than they are in the image of the parties and their leaders.' How far do you agree with this view? [30]

→

A-level

1 Evaluate the extent to which the media influence the outcome of elections in the UK. [30]

2 Evaluate the extent to which election campaigns influence the outcome of the vote. [30]

3 Using the source, evaluate the extent to which party leaders can secure victory in elections. [30]

Not surprisingly, the media tend to concentrate upon the leaders of the main parties during election campaigns. It is easier to attract the attention of their readers with human interest stories than with dry party manifestos. There is no doubt that leaders are an important factor in voting behaviour, but their influence has probably been exaggerated.

A proportion of the electorate still feel a strong attachment to a party, even in spite of partisan dealignment, so the way they vote is highly predictable. For those with no such strong attachment, valence is important. This concerns how people feel about a party, whether it is competent, whether it can be trusted, especially over the economy, and whether it is united. Leadership qualities are part of valence, to be sure, but they are rarely decisive.

Positive and negative images of leaders have always played a part, of course. Gordon Brown lost in 2010 partly as a result of his poor media image. Margaret Thatcher, in the 1980s, probably enhanced her party's majorities as a result of her positive image as the 'iron lady'. The 2017 general election was largely fought as a contest between Theresa May, representing 'strong and stable' government, and Jeremy Corbyn, who was portrayed in much of the press as weak and indecisive. It is likely that the press would like us to believe that they are influencing the outcome of elections by highlighting the strengths and weaknesses of party leaders, but the truth is rarely so simple. This was never more clearly demonstrated than in the June 2017 general election when Jeremy Corbyn defied a storm of press ridicule and opposition to enhance the reputation of both himself and his party.

Demographic factors, the issues and the image of the parties would seem to be more important, according to most experts on electoral activity. It is also true that social media are gradually taking over from the traditional newspapers as voters' principal source of opinion and information.

Source: original material

In your response you must:
● compare the different opinions in the source
● consider this view and the alternative to this view in a balanced way
● use knowledge and understanding to help you analyse and evaluate.

Answers and quick quiz 4 online

ONLINE

Summary

You should now have an understanding of:
● the influence of class on voting behaviour
● the influence of demographic factors on voting behaviour
● the influence of factors other than class and demographics on voting behaviour
● the key aspects of at least three general elections which can explain the outcome
● the role of the media in elections
● how opinion polls work
● the impact of opinion polls on election outcomes.

5 The constitution

What is a constitution?

REVISED

A **constitution** in politics can be described as a set of rules which regulates the system of government and politics of a country. It has the following functions:

- It establishes the distribution of power within the state.
- In so doing it also establishes the relationships between the institutions that make up the state.
- It establishes the limits of government power.
- It asserts the rights of the citizens and how these may be protected
- It describes how the constitution itself can be amended – what the procedure is for such a process.

> **Constitution** A set of rules that establishes a country's governmental and political system.

The development of the UK Constitution

REVISED

The UK Constitution has developed over many centuries. The reasons for its slow, gradual development are twofold:

1. It is known as an **organic constitution** which has been shaped by gradual changes in UK society and politics. It has never been imposed on the UK at a single event.
2. There has never been an historical event, such as a revolution, which has overturned the existing order and therefore heralded in a new political order. In the civil war and Commonwealth period of 1642–60, the monarchy was replaced by parliamentary government and later by dictatorship (of Oliver Cromwell). All attempts to write a constitution failed, so monarchy was restored.

> **Organic constitution** A political constitution that has developed naturally in accordance with changes in the nature of society and the political system, as opposed to a constitution which is created at one historical moment in time.

Table 5.1 shows the main stages in the development of the UK Constitution.

Table 5.1 Stages in the development of the UK Constitution

Historical event	Description
Magna Carta, 1215	An agreement between the nobles and the king. It established the principle of the rule of law, i.e. that government must operate within the law and the law should apply equally to all citizens.
Bill of Rights, 1689	An agreement between the king and Parliament. It first established the idea of the sovereignty of Parliament over the king in matters of legislation.
Act of Settlement, 1701	Established the monarch's position as ruler of England, Scotland, Wales and Ireland. It also established that the rules of succession to the throne should be determined by Parliament.
Act of Union, 1707	Dissolved the Scottish Parliament and established the union of Great Britain and Ireland.
Parliament Acts, 1911 and 1949	Limited the power of the House of Lords to delaying legislation for one year and took away the house's power over financial matters.
European Communities Act, 1972	Established the UK's entry into the European Community (EU)
European (Notification of Withdrawal) Act, 2017	Gave parliamentary approval to the UK's decision to leave the European Union.

Exam practice answers and quick quizzes at **www.hoddereducation.co.uk/myrevisionnotesdownloads**

The nature and principles of the UK Constitution

The main principles of constitutions in general, and concepts relating to them, are as follows.

Codification

- When a constitution can be found in one single document and so has one single source.
- When constitutional laws are clearly separate from ordinary, non-constitutional laws.
- Constitutional laws are seen as superior to ordinary laws.
- Constitutional laws are subject to a separate set of procedures for amendment to ordinary laws.
- Most modern states have **codified constitutions**, such as the USA (1787) and France (1958).

Entrenchment

- This is a principle closely linked to codification.
- With an **entrenched constitution**, there are special procedures which make it more difficult to amend constitutional laws than ordinary laws.
- The constitutional principles of a country are protected by some kind of supreme constitutional court.
- Examples of entrenchment methods are the USA (approval of two thirds of Congress and three-quarters of the 50 states) and Ireland (by referendum).

Exam tip

You should not separate the concepts of a codified and an entrenched constitution. If the UK were to adopt a codified constitution it would also have to be entrenched. If it were not entrenched, codifying the constitution would be futile as it could be changed by any future Parliament. A codified constitution would only be effective it were safeguarded in some way as constitutions are in the USA (by an enhanced congressional majority and three-quarters state support) and France (by referendum).

Uncodified constitutions

- A constitution which does not have a single source and is not contained in a single document.
- Such constitutions have not been created at one single point in time.
- Although there is no single document, this does not mean that there is no constitution, simply that the constitutional rules are more difficult to establish.
- **Uncodified constitutions** are flexible and can easily be changed, so they are **unentrenched**.

Sovereignty

- Legal sovereignty refers to the location of ultimate power.
- Legal sovereignty also means the location of the source of all political power.
- There is no higher political authority than where legal sovereignty lies.

Codified constitution A constitution which is set out in a single document and has a single source.

Entrenched constitution An entrenched constitution has special arrangements to safeguard it from being amended by a temporary government or legislature.

Uncodified constitution A constitution which is not contained in a single document and has a number of different sources.

Unentrenched constitution An unentrenched constitution can be amended by an individual government or Parliament.

Typical mistake

In exams some students refer to the UK Constitution as 'unwritten'. This is misleading. The constitution is partly written (e.g. constitutional statutes, the European Convention on Human Rights) and partly unwritten (conventions). It is more accurate to describe the constitution as 'uncodified'.

- Political sovereignty refers to the location of *real* power.
- External sovereignty refers to the recognition of the right of the regime to govern a country, as granted by other countries.
- **Parliamentary sovereignty** means that legal sovereignty lies only with the UK Parliament.

> **Typical mistake**
>
> Although the reigning monarch is often referred to as 'the sovereign', you should ignore this use of the term 'sovereign'. Only the UK Parliament is sovereign. You should discount the possibility that a UK monarch would ever try to exercise sovereignty, which exists only in theory.

Unitary constitution

- A system of government where legal sovereignty lies in one place, usually either a constitution or a central legislature.
- In **unitary constitutions**, power can be delegated to subsidiary bodies, but this power can be returned to the sovereign body.
- The UK Constitution is a prominent example of a unitary constitution, as is that of France.

Federal constitution

- A system of government where legal power is divided between a central authority and regional authorities.
- In **federal constitutions**, the division of powers reserved to regional bodies is symmetrical, i.e. they all have equal powers.
- The powers of the regional bodies are protected by an entrenched constitution.

Separation of powers

- A constitutional principle common to most codified constitutions. The powers of the different branches of government are clearly defined and separated.
- This means that the different branches control each other's power.
- The opposite is the fusion of powers, as applies in the UK.

The UK Constitution has the following characteristics:
- It is uncodified.
- It is not entrenched.
- Nevertheless, the **rule of law** applies.
- It is unitary.
- The powers of the legislature and executive are fused.
- It is organic and develops naturally.

> **Exam tip**
>
> It is useful to distinguish constitutional principles which exist *in theory* (*de jure*) and those which exist *in practice* (*de facto*). Thus devolution grants sovereignty to Scotland *de facto* but not *de jure* because it was confirmed by a referendum; the monarch could refuse royal assent to legislation *de jure* but not *de facto*; the UK Parliament can dismiss a government in theory but this will rarely happen in practice.

Parliamentary sovereignty
The principle in the UK that the Westminster Parliament claims to hold legal sovereignty and no other body can claim such sovereignty.

Unitary constitution
A constitution which establishes that legal sovereignty resides in one location.

Federal constitution A constitution where legal sovereignty is divided between the central government and regional governments.

Rule of law The principle that all citizens are equal under the law and that the government itself is subject to the same laws as the citizens. Government is not above the law.

> **Typical mistake**
>
> Many students confuse power with sovereignty. This is potentially dangerous. Sovereignty refers to ultimate power which cannot be overruled by any individual, institution or constitution. Power, meanwhile, is a slightly weaker expression. It means the ability to take certain actions but it could, in theory, be overruled by a higher authority. Thus the UK Parliament is *sovereign*, but the prime minister has considerable *power*.

The sources of the UK Constitution

Because the UK Constitution is not codified, it has several different sources. Table 5.2 shows these sources, with examples.

Table 5.2 The sources of the UK Constitution

Source	Description	Examples
Parliamentary statutes	Laws passed by Parliament	Human Rights Act 1998 Constitutional Reform Act 2005
Constitutional conventions	Unwritten rules which are considered to be binding on all members of the political community	Salisbury Convention Collective cabinet responsibility
Foreign treaties and agreements	Agreements with external bodies that bind the UK in some way	Maastricht Treaty with the EU (until 2019) European Convention on Human Rights with the Council of Europe
Authoritative works	The writings of constitutional experts that clarify the meaning of the constitution	A. V. Dicey's *Law of the Constitution* Walter Bagehot's *The English Constitution*
Common law and tradition	Rules that have been passed down through various judgments in court cases	The rules of parliamentary procedure and discipline Various rights such as freedom of expression

Parliamentary statutes Any law that has been passed by the UK Parliament and has received royal assent

Authoritative works Historical books and documents that clarify the meaning of constitutional principles.

Common law Unwritten laws that are not passed by Parliament but have passed down through history in the form of judicial precedents.

Now test yourself

1 Look at these sources of the UK Constitution. In each case, identify two examples. (In the case of an external treaty, only one of these will operate after 2019.)

Constitutional source	Examples	
Parliamentary statute		
Work of authority		
Convention		
Common law and tradition		
External treaty or agreement		

2 Identify two countries that have codified constitutions and one, other than the UK, that does not.

Answers on p. 125

Constitutional reform, 1997–2010

REVISED

The purposes of constitutional reform in this period were fourfold:

- The political system needed to be more democratic.
- The political system was too centralised, with too much power in too few hands.
- Citizens' rights were inadequately protected.
- The political system needed to be modernised and brought into line with other modern democracies.

Table 5.3 indicates the key constitutional reforms made between 1997 and 2010. They were all made by Labour governments.

Table 5.3 Constitutional reform, 1997–2010

Reform	Effect
Devolution, 1997–98	The transfer of extensive powers away from Westminster and Whitehall to governments and elected assemblies in Scotland, Wales and Northern Ireland.
	At the same time, new electoral systems were introduced in the three countries — the additional member system in Scotland and Wales and the single transferable vote in Northern Ireland.
Human Rights Act 1998	This brought the European Convention on Human Rights into UK law. It is binding on all bodies except the UK Parliament.
House of Lords Act 1999	This removed the voting rights of hundreds of hereditary peers in the House of Lords — 92 hereditary peers were allowed to retain their rights. The rest of the House of Lords was made up of Church of England bishops and appointed peers.
Greater London Authority Act 1999	This introduced an elected mayor for London with extensive powers over, for example, planning, policing, social housing, emergency services, tourism and arts funding.
Freedom of Information Act 2000	This granted the legal right to individuals and organisations to access official information held by all public bodies, except for information concerning national security.
Constitutional Reform Act 2005	This took the 12 most senior judges out of the House of Lords and created instead the Supreme Court, the highest court of appeal and legal interpretation in the country.
	It also guaranteed the independence of the judiciary, took the appointment of judges out of political hands and replaced the Lord Chancellor, a cabinet minister, as head of the judiciary by the Lord Chief Justice, a senior judge.
Backbench Business Committee 2010	A new backbench committee in the Commons was given control of 35 days for debate chosen by backbenchers and not the government.
The increased use of referendums	This is not a single event but the principle was established that important constitutional changes needed to be approved and entrenched by a referendum.

Governments in the period were committed to other reforms but these were not implemented:

- the replacement of the House of Lords with an elected second chamber
- the introduction of proportional representation for general elections (if approved by referendum)
- the codification of the powers of the prime minister in relation to Parliament.

Constitutional reform, 2010–15

REVISED

The coalition government in this period was committed to some reforms, largely under the influence of the Liberal Democrats, who shared power with the Conservatives. Table 5.4 describes the key reforms in this period.

Table 5.4 Constitutional reform, 2010–15

Reform	Effect
Fixed-term Parliaments Act 2011	The dates of general elections were taken out of the control of the prime minister. Elections are to take place every five years. An early election can be called if approved by a two-thirds majority of the House of Commons, or if the government loses a vote of no confidence.
Wales Act 2014	A limited extension of devolution to Wales, this gave the Welsh government limited powers to raise new forms of tax and to control the revenue from them. It provided for a referendum in Wales to determine whether the country should have some devolved power over income tax rates and revenues.
Recall of MPs Act 2015	This gives constituents the power to order their MP to face a by-election if he or she has been guilty of serious misconduct.

Constitutional reform since 2015

REVISED

The Conservative government which came to power in 2015 renewed its interest in constitutional reform, with everything overshadowed by the prospect of the UK leaving the EU. Table 5.5 outlines the reforms instituted since 2015.

Table 5.5 Constitutional reform since 2015

Reform	Effect
Order allowing Wales to take control over income tax revenue, 2015	After 2019 the Welsh Assembly will be able to claim control over income tax revenue raised in Wales.
Scotland Act 2016	This increased the devolved powers of the Scottish government and Parliament. These included welfare provision and the levels of a number of social security benefits. It also granted power to set the rates of income tax in Scotland and to determine how the receipts from income tax should be spent. In addition, the Scottish government will have control over half the proceeds of VAT raised in Scotland. The Act also made devolution permanent, though this remains subject to the sovereignty of the UK Parliament.

→

Reform	Effect
Wales Act 2017	Wales can determine its own electoral system (though not for general elections).
	The Welsh Assembly may turn itself into a parliament and may take on limited law-making functions.
	Increased powers over various public services were also devolved.
European Union (Notification of Withdrawal) Act 2017	This is the Act of Parliament giving notice of the UK's intention to leave the EU in March 2019.
The election of mayors in various cities and regions, 2017	In six cities and regions mayors are to be elected with varying degrees of independent power, such as over planning, transport, housing and policing.
English Votes for English Laws (EVEL) 2017	A new parliamentary procedure will be introduced whereby MPs sitting for Welsh, Scottish and Northern Ireland seats will not debate or vote on issues affecting only England.

The objectives of constitutional reform since 2010 have been:
- mainly to decentralise power away from London and central government
- to make elections fairer
- to guarantee the UK's withdrawal from the EU in accordance with the result of the 2016 referendum.

> **Exam tip**
>
> Make sure you know which constitutional reforms occurred between 1997 and 2010, which occurred between 2010 and 2015 and which have occurred since 2015. When asking questions about constitutional reforms in the UK, the examiners usually specify a certain period. You therefore need to know which reforms can be included in your answer and which can be excluded.

Now test yourself

TESTED

3 Look at these post-1997 constitutional reforms. Which government enacted them? (You may need to refer back to the general election summaries in Chapter 3.) The first answer is given for you.

Reform	Government
Human Rights Act	Labour 1997–2001
Fixed-term Parliaments Act	
Constitutional Reform Act	
House of Lords Act	
Freedom of Information Act	
English Votes for English Laws Order	

4 Outline three parliamentary reforms made since 1997.

Answers on p. 125

The nature of devolution

REVISED

Devolution in the UK has the following features:

- It is the transfer of powers but not sovereignty to the three national regions of the UK.
- Originally the funding for devolved services came from a central government annual grant, but increasingly the devolved governments have had independent control over taxes raised in their countries.
- The size of the devolution grants has been calculated using the 'Barnett formula', which takes account of the fact that the three countries have greater needs than England.
- It is asymmetrical, meaning that the three regions have not been granted the same powers.
- The devolved administrations each have an elected assembly (parliament in Scotland) and an executive, or government, which is drawn from the assembly.
- The method of election of the assemblies is not first-past-the-post but by forms of proportional representation.
- In general, devolution has been entrenched by referendums.
- The UK Parliament has the option of bringing back the powers to Westminster and has suspended devolved government in Northern Ireland several times.

The distinctions between devolution and federalism are as follows:

- Federalism distributes legal sovereignty to regional governments, whereas devolution only distributes power.
- Federalism distributes power symmetrically (all regional governments have the same powers), whereas devolution in the UK is asymmetrical.
- Federal arrangements are entrenched by a constitution, whereas devolution is not legally entrenched.
- Therefore, federated powers rarely change, whereas devolution is an ongoing process.

> **Devolution** A process whereby power, but not legal sovereignty, is distributed away from central government to regional governments.

Revision activity

Revise examples of powers that were and are:
1 Exclusive to the Scottish administration.
2 Applicable throughout the UK.
3 Exclusive to England.
4 Granted to the Northern Ireland government in 1998 in order to promote peace.

Devolution in England

REVISED

There is no devolution in England, i.e. to English regions, in the same sense that there is devolution to Scotland, Wales and Northern Ireland. The key features of such devolution in England are as follows:

- In 2004 a referendum was held in Northeast England to gauge support for regional devolution of powers. However, this was rejected by 77% of the voters.
- Powers were devolved to a London mayor and assembly in 1999. These include powers over planning, social housing, arts subsidies, public transport, policing and emergency services.

- Considerable powers were devolved to Manchester in 2017. These are similar to the powers of the London mayor but also include powers over NHS spending in the region.
- Also in 2017 powers were devolved to a number of cities and regions, administered by an elected mayor. The devolved powers vary from one region to another.

Devolution in Scotland

The context of devolution in Scotland includes the following features:
- Scottish government had long enjoyed some autonomous powers, notably over education and law and order. The country had its own legal system and civil service.
- An original attempt to introduce devolution in 1979 failed because there was inadequate support in the country.
- Nationalist sentiment increased during the 1990s, persuading the Labour government to include the measure in its 1997 referendum.
- A referendum in 1997 approved devolution in Scotland, with a majority of 74–26%.
- Nationalist sentiment continued to grow and the Scottish National Party made gradual progress in winning seats in the Scottish Parliament, securing an overall majority in 2011.
- Scottish independence was rejected in a 2014 referendum by 55–45%. However, the outcome was so close that all major UK parties promised to increase devolved powers.
- The Scottish National Party won 56 out of the 59 seats in Scotland in the 2015 general election, putting further pressure on UK parties.
- The 2016 Scotland Act granted enhanced powers to Scottish government.
- The Scottish Nationalists have continued to press for a fresh independence referendum as in 2016 the majority of Scots voted to remain in the EU. They are also pressing for the devolution of more powers.

The Scottish Parliament and government have control over the following areas of government responsibility:
- agriculture, forestry and fisheries
- education and training
- environment
- health and social services
- housing
- law and order (including policing)
- local government
- sport and the arts
- tourism and economic development
- local transport
- a range of welfare and social security benefits.

In addition, from 2017, the Scottish government enjoyed considerable financial autonomy. It:
- can determine income tax rates
- has control over receipts from income tax
- controls half the revenue from VAT collected in Scotland
- has control over revenue from air passenger duty and other minor taxes collected in Scotland.

Other features of devolved administration in Scotland are as follows:

- The Scottish Parliament is elected using the additional member system, a hybrid of first-past-the-post and the regional list system.
- The Scottish Executive is drawn from the Scottish Parliament, whether it is a majority government, minority government or coalition.
- The first minister is the leader of the biggest party in the Scottish Parliament.

Devolution in Wales

The context of devolution in Wales includes the following features:

- Unlike Scotland, Wales had no tradition of autonomous powers — it had always been governed from London.
- An original attempt to introduce devolution in 1979 failed when the vast majority of Welsh voters rejected the proposal.
- Nationalist sentiment increased slightly during the 1990s but the main reason for the proposal was that the Labour government decided that devolution had to be offered to Wales as it was being offered to Scotland.
- A referendum in 1997 approved devolution in Wales, though by a tiny majority only on a low turnout. In view of the lack of enthusiasm, it was proposed that only modest powers would be transferred.
- As devolved powers grew in Scotland, Wales was offered a similar extension to its own powers.
- A referendum in 2011 saw 63% of Welsh voters approving the introduction of some law-making powers to the Welsh Assembly.

The Welsh Assembly and government have control over the following key areas of government responsibility (in 2017). This is not a complete list but contains important powers:

- agriculture, fisheries, forestry and rural development
- ancient monuments and historical buildings
- culture
- economic development
- education and training
- environment
- fire and rescue services and promotion of fire safety
- food
- health and health services
- highways and transport
- housing
- local government
- social welfare
- sport and recreation
- tourism
- town and country planning
- water and flood defences
- Welsh language.

Other features of devolved administration in Wales are as follows:

- The Welsh National Assembly is elected using the additional member system, a hybrid of first-past-the-post and the regional list system.
- The Welsh Executive is drawn from the assembly, whether it is a majority government, minority government or coalition.
- The first minister is the leader of the biggest party in the Welsh Assembly.

Devolution in Northern Ireland

The context of devolution in Northern Ireland includes the following features:

- The main context is the long history of sectarian conflict in the province since the 1970s between the nationalists, who supported a united Ireland, and unionists, who wished to remain part of the United Kingdom.
- From 1993 a peace process began, so both the Conservative government of John Major and the new Labour government after 1997 wished to reinforce that process.
- It was hoped that if there were to be autonomous government in Northern Ireland, the province might be able to solve its own problems rather than rely on the UK government, which was not seen as neutral.
- The devolution plan was to introduce a proportional representation system (STV) for elections to give a fair chance for all sections of a fragmented society to gain representation.
- The system devised promised a power-sharing government in which all significant parties would be guaranteed ministerial posts.
- It was hoped that a power-sharing coalition government would prevent a return to conflict.

The Northern Ireland Assembly and government have control over the following key areas of government responsibility (in 2017). This is not a complete list but contains important powers:

- agriculture, environment and rural affairs
- communities
- economy
- education
- finance
- health
- infrastructure
- justice and policing.

Now test yourself

TESTED

5 Look at these powers. Which countries of the UK, not including England, had these powers in 2017?

Power	Countries
Health care administration	
Criminal laws	
Income tax levels	
Education	

6 Outline the taxation powers of Scottish government.

Answers on p. 125

The future of devolution

REVISED

Various issues remain concerning the future of devolution:
- The issue of regional devolution in England remains active. The Conservative Party is hoping to decentralise power within England.

- Scottish devolution is still being debated. If the Scots do not achieve independence in the near future, there will be continued demands for further devolution (known as 'devo-max').
- Devo-max in Scotland would entail the transfer of virtually all government powers, with the exception of defence, foreign, economic and financial policy.
- The prospects for further Welsh devolution remain modest as nationalist feeling in the country is still weak.
- The main significant issue remaining is whether there should be English devolution.

English devolution

This concerns the debate over whether there should be a separate English Parliament to deal with matters that concern *only* England, such as health and education. In the meantime, a principle known as EVEL (English Votes for English Laws) has been instituted. The rules of EVEL are as follows:

- All bills are considered in the normal way by all MPs.
- The Speaker of the House of Commons rules on whether a matter to be debated concerns only England.
- If it is an England-only matter, there is a debate only among English MPs.
- Bills must be approved *both* by the whole House and by the MPs sitting for English constituencies.

Further developments of English devolution are possible:

- A completely separate English Parliament could be elected and sit alongside the UK Parliament.
- This would be full English devolution. There would also be separate English and UK governments.
- In theory, a different party could be in control of England from the government in control of the UK as a whole.
- It is extremely unlikely in the foreseeable future that such an arrangement will be introduced.

> **Typical mistake**
>
> Devolution is a process and not an event. You should consider devolution as a long-term exercise, where the distribution of power between the countries of the UK is in a constant state of change.

The codification debate

REVISED

The arguments as to whether the UK Constitution should be codified are balanced. They are outlined in Table 5.6.

Table 5.6 The codification debate

Arguments in favour of codifying the constitution	Arguments against codifying the constitution
It would prevent the creeping increase in executive power.	The UK would lose flexibility in its constitutional arrangements.
It would help to improve the safeguarding of rights.	Excessive protection of rights might reduce the government's ability to protect national security.
It would educate the people about the way in which government and the political system work.	It would be difficult and time consuming to organise the codifying of a constitution and to organise public approval.
It would safeguard the devolution of power to the national regions.	A codified constitution like that of the USA might thrust the Supreme Court into political issues and so threaten its neutrality and independence.

Revision activity

Make sure you thoroughly revise:
1 Three arguments in favour of introducing a codified UK Constitution.
2 Three arguments against introducing a codified UK Constitution.
3 Three possible ways in which a codified constitution could be entrenched in the UK.

Exam practice

AS

1 Describe the main features of a codified constitution. [10]
2 Describe the main features of the Constitutional Reform Act of 2005. [10]
3 Using the source, explain why the Labour government instituted a programme of constitutional reform. [10]

The Labour government which came to power in 1997 was committed to four main objectives in its constitutional reform programme. First, it hoped to improve the quality of democracy in the UK. Second, it believed that power was too centralised and should therefore be more dispersed. Third, the new government believed that rights were inadequately protected and promoted in the UK. Finally, and more generally, it wanted to modernise the old traditional constitution, bringing it into line with other modern democracies in the world.

The jewel in the crown was undoubtedly devolution. Here, however, modernisation and democratisation were not the only objectives. The rise in nationalism, which had been growing in Scotland and Wales in the 1990s, had reached such proportions that the break-up of the United Kingdom was being predicted. So, in the hope of heading off nationalist sentiment, the Labour leadership decided that significant powers should be devolved to Scotland and Wales. This, it was expected, would be enough to reduce the influence of the nationalists. In Northern Ireland, meanwhile, devolution was seen as one of the measures needed to safeguard the fragile peace which had come to the province in the mid-1990s.

Source: original material

In your response you must use knowledge and understanding to analyse points that are only in the source. You will **not** be rewarded for introducing any additional points that are not in the source.

4 'The idea of parliamentary sovereignty is now outdated in the UK.' How far do you agree with this view of the UK's political system? [30]

A-level

1 Evaluate the extent to which the devolution process has successfully enhanced democracy in the UK.   [30]
2 Evaluate the extent to which the UK is now effectively a federal system.   [30]
3 Using the source, evaluate the arguments for introducing a codified constitution for the UK.   [30]

There are a number of reasons why the introduction of a codified constitution remains an objective of liberal-minded politicians and constitutional experts. Apart from the obvious argument that the UK is out of step with virtually the whole of the rest of the democratic world, there are a number of recent developments which have brought the issue to prominence.

Above all, the devolution process has created a patchwork of overlapping and confusing powers which are dispersed among the four nations of the UK and to the big cities and even some geographical regions. It may, therefore, be time to codify the ways in which such powers are distributed. In addition, the whole status of referendums (increasingly used) needs to be clarified. Are they binding or are they not? On a broader level, we can ask the question of whether it is realistic today to view the UK Parliament as sovereign. If it is not, in reality, sovereign, then we need to clarify where sovereignty lies. The return of sovereignty after Brexit, too, presents a need to clarify this issue. There are also the older arguments that the constitution should be codified to protect citizens' rights more effectively and to prevent the creeping increase in unchecked executive power.

Nevertheless, critics argue that these arguments are outweighed by other considerations. We would, for example, be exchanging the known for the unknown, something that conservatives are instinctively concerned about. Above all, however, it is the flexibility of the UK's ancient uncodified constitution that exercises the minds of such critics most vigorously. 'We do not want,' they argue, 'to find ourselves in a position like that of the USA, where the entrenched and codified constitution acts as a block on many important reforms such as changes to the gun laws and socialised health care.' Our flexible constitution, they add, is a strength, not a weakness.

Source: original material

In your response you must:
● compare the different opinions in the source
● consider this view and the alternative to this view in a balanced way
● use knowledge and understanding to help you analyse and evaluate.

Answers and quick quiz 5 online

ONLINE

Summary

You should now have an understanding of:
● the distinction between codified and uncodified constitutions
● the distinction between a unitary and a federal constitution
● the main concepts related to constitutionalism
● how the UK Constitution has developed in order to illustrate an understanding of its main characteristics
● constitutional reform since 1997 and the main effects of these reforms

● the concept of sovereignty — you will be able to analyse and evaluate debates about where it is now located in the UK
● the nature of devolution
● how devolution affects different parts of the UK in different ways — you will be able to evaluate its success or failure
● debates about future constitutional reform issues
● whether the UK should have a codified constitution.

6 Parliament

The structure of the House of Commons

The House of Commons is known as the 'lower house' and is the elected half of **Parliament**. The structure of the House of Commons is as follows:

- **650 Members of Parliament** (soon to be reduced, probably to 600) elected from constituencies throughout the UK.
- **Candidates** for such elections are selected by committees drawn from local constituency parties.
- **Frontbench MPs** — government ministers, senior and junior, plus leading spokespersons from opposition parties (about 150).
- **Backbench MPs** — all those MPs who are not frontbenchers (about 500).
- **Select committees** — permanent committees of backbench MPs, elected by all the MPs. They have various roles, including calling government to account. Select committees have mostly between 11 and 15 members each.
- **Legislative committees** (also called bill committees) — temporary committees which scrutinise proposed legislation and propose amendments to improve the legislation. They mostly have 20–40 members.
- **Party whips** — senior MPs whose role is to keep party discipline, inform MPs about parliamentary business and occasionally discipline dissident MPs.
- **The Speaker** — he or she is elected by MPs, is neutral and keeps order in the house as well as ruling on various disputes that arise over the order and nature of business running through the House.

> **Parliament** A name given to the legislature in many countries. This means it has the dual role of legitimising proposed legislation and representing the people.

> **Typical mistake**
>
> It is often believed that the term 'legislature' means a 'law-making body', so the UK Parliament must make law. This is misleading. Parliament does not make law (with the exception of rare private members' bills) — laws are developed and drafted by government. What Parliament is doing is scrutinising and legitimising laws, granting consent to them on behalf of the people, not making them.

The structure of the House of Lords

The House of Lords is known as the 'upper house' and is the unelected half of Parliament. It contains about 800 peers. The following types of peers sit in the House of Lords:

- **Hereditary peers.** They have inherited the title from their father and will pass their peerage on to their sons (a few daughters). There are normally 92 of these peers.
- **Life peers.** Appointed for life by party leaders and an Appointments Commission, they do not pass on their title to their children. These are a mixture of former politicians and civil servants, other prominent citizens, often retired, political appointees and experts in various fields.
- **Archbishops and bishops of the Church of England.** There are 26 of these. No other religions have automatic representation.
- **The Lord Speaker.** He or she presides over debates in the house and maintains discipline.

Peers fall into three main categories:
- professional politicians (including some government ministers), who are appointed to be working peers and who are party members, expected to support the party on most occasions

- amateur peers, who are not politicians but may nevertheless support a particular party
- crossbench peers, who have no party allegiance and so are fully independent.

MPs

MPs all sit for a constituency. You should know the following key points about MPs:

- MPs who are not members of the government or the leadership of their party are known as **backbenchers**.
- They virtually all represent a political party. So-called 'independent' MPs have sat in the past, but these are rare.
- To be a party candidate it is necessary to be 'adopted' by a party.
- Most parties adopt candidates through local party committees, which draw up a shortlist and interview potential candidates.
- A candidate will win a parliamentary seat if he or she wins the most votes in a general or by-election through the first-past-the-post electoral system.
- MPs enjoy **parliamentary privilege**. This means they are free from outside interference and cannot be prosecuted or sued for anything they say within the House of Commons.
- MPs who misbehave or commit serious crimes may be suspended from the Chamber and, in some circumstances, can be forced by their constituents to face a by-election.
- MPs may seek to be elected to be a member of a select committee and are required by the party whips to sit regularly on legislative committees.
- If an MP wishes to speak in a debate, they must indicate this desire to their party whips and to the Speaker.

Backbenchers MPs and peers who are not senior members of their party and so sit in Parliament behind the front bench.

Parliamentary privilege An ancient principle that protects MPs from external pressure and specifically means they cannot be prosecuted or sued for anything they may say in the House of Commons. It also implies that the monarch can never interfere with the work of the UK Parliament.

Peers

There are several ways an individual may become a member of the House of Lords:

- Twenty-six senior bishops and archbishops of the Church of England are entitled to sit in the Lords.
- Hereditary peers may apply to be elected by all other hereditary peers to the House of Lords. The maximum number of such peers is 92.
- Party leaders regularly nominate people to become **life peers**. These may be former politicians, civil servants, or prominent citizens who have led important organisations and have special expertise and experience. Most such nominations are party members.
- Organisations may also nominate potential peers and these are vetted by the Appointments Commission, which may grant peerages. Most such life peers are independent crossbenchers.

Life peer A person who is granted a peerage for life but cannot pass that peerage on to their successors.

Peers have the following roles:

- Representing sections of society in Parliament, ensuring that their interests are taken account of — examples of sections of society represented are ethnic minorities, the elderly, hospital patients, the professions.
- Representing important political causes, ensuring they are given as much publicity as possible. These are typically environmental issues, human rights concerns and animal welfare.

Exam tip

Remember to distinguish between the UK Parliament, which you may describe as 'Westminster', and the Scottish Parliament. Always refer to the UK Parliament *or* Westminster.

- Scrutinising legislation. Peers with special expertise play a valuable role in examining proposed legislation.
- Every government department has a frontbench representative in the Lords. This gives peers the opportunity to call government to account, though this function receives less publicity than its equivalent activity in the Commons.
- Many peers sit on committees that investigate aspects of government policy and produce reports which may be critical or supportive and may suggest changes to proposals.

Table 6.1 shows some prominent peers, their party allegiance and their fields of expertise.

Table 6.1 Prominent peers

Peer	Party	Field of expertise
Lord Adonis	Crossbencher (formerly Labour)	Transport and education
Lord Winston	Labour	Infertility and medical ethics
Lord Dannatt	Crossbencher	Military issues
Baroness Chakrabarti	Labour	Human rights
Baroness Warsi	Conservative	Race relations

Typical mistake

Students often become confused by the fact that government ministers sit in the House of Commons and, less often, the House of Lords. This is because ministers have two roles — they are MPs or peers as well as being ministers. Of course, their ministerial role nearly always takes precedence.

Now test yourself

TESTED

1 Look at these descriptions of members of the Houses of Commons and Lords. In each case, who is being described?

Power	Who is being described
An MP who presides over debates in the House of Commons	
A party official who seeks to ensure that MPs or peers who represent a party vote according to the wishes of the party leadership	
An appointed member in the House of Lords who does not have any party allegiance	
The person, a member of the opposition, who presides over a committee that examines the financial arrangements of the government	

2 Outline the role of the Public Accounts Committee.

Answers on p. 126

Functions of the House of Commons

The House of Commons has the following functions:
- **Legitimation.** This is the formal process of making proposed laws legitimate by granting consent. In a sense the Commons is granting consent on behalf of the people. In extreme circumstances the Commons may reject legislation altogether.
- **Accountability.** This key aspect sees the Commons again acting on behalf of the people. Making government accountable means criticising, forcing ministers to explain policy and perhaps even dismissing a government through a vote of no **confidence**.
- **Scrutiny.** Any proposed legislation is examined by MPs. They may make amendments to improve the legislation and to protect the interests of minorities.
- **Constituency work.** MPs are expected to ensure that the interests of their constituencies are protected – both the constituency as a whole and individual constituents.
- **Representation of interests.** When the interests of sections of society may be affected by policy, proposed legislation and government decisions, groups of MPs may seek to protect their interests.
- **National debate.** Sometimes great issues need to be debated by the people's representatives. MPs have opportunities to debate such issues.

Confidence The term is usually applied to a vote (or motion) of no confidence. If such a vote is passed, it will effectively dismiss the government and force an election. If a vote of no confidence is defeated, it implies that Parliament has confidence in the government of the day.

Functions of the House of Lords

These are more limited than those of the House of Commons:
- **Revising.** This is a shared function with the House of Commons. The Lords scrutinises legislation carefully. The fact that the House contains so many experts makes this process especially meaningful.
- **Delaying.** The Lords cannot veto a piece of legislation but they can force the government to re-present it the following year. This effectively forces government to think again for a year and possibly add amendments to make the legislation acceptable.
- **Secondary legislation.** There is a great deal of minor regulation within major laws which has to be approved. The Commons does not have time to review it all, so the Lords spends its greater available time checking that it is acceptable.
- **National debate.** This is a function the Lords shares with the House of Commons, though its deliberations are less influential.

Powers of the House of Commons

The House of Commons has the power to:
- approve or reject proposed legislation
- dismiss a government through a vote of no confidence
- order ministers to answer questions on the floor of the house, in select committee or in writing
- amend legislation
- order debates on important national issues or in a crisis or emergency
- introduce matters of concern to an MP in a **ten-minute rule debate** or an **adjournment debate**.

Backbench MPs may introduce private members' bills for consideration.

Ten-minute rule debate A regular opportunity for backbench MPs to raise an issue of importance to them. MPs have ten minutes to explain their concern.

Adjournment debate When Parliament has some spare time at the end of a debate, backbenchers are given the limited opportunity to raise an issue of importance to them.

Powers of the House of Lords

The House of Lords has the power to:
- delay the passage of legislation for at least a year
- amend legislation, though such amendments may be overturned in the House of Commons
- order government ministers (who must also be members of the House of Lords) to answer questions on government policies and decisions
- debate issues of great national concern.

Distinctions between the House of Commons and the House of Lords

The key distinctions are as follows:
- The House of Commons can veto proposed legislation whereas the Lords can only delay legislation for a year.
- The House of Commons can amend legislation whereas the Lords can only propose amendments which may be rejected by the House of Commons.
- The House of Commons can call ministers and government representatives to account in select committees. No such committees exist in the House of Lords.
- The House of Commons can dismiss a government by passing a vote of no confidence. The Lords cannot do this.
- In general terms, the Commons has **democratic legitimacy** while the Lords has no such legitimacy.

Democratic legitimacy The authority a body gains if it is elected and accountable to the people.

Revision activity

Revise examples of roles possibly played more effectively by the House of Lords than the House of Commons. These should be in the following areas:
1 Legislation.
2 Minorities.
3 Debates.

Typical mistake

There is a temptation to see the monarch as part of Parliament because of the State Opening of Parliament, the annual Queen's Speech and the requirement that all bills must receive royal assent to become law. This is misleading. The monarch's role is purely non-political and passive. The monarchy plays no meaningful part in the legislating process.

Debates about parliamentary powers

You need to assess the effectiveness of Parliament. The key issues, showing strengths and weaknesses of Parliament in general, are shown in Table 6.2.

Table 6.2 An assessment of the effectiveness of Parliament

Role	Positive aspects	Negative aspects
Holding government to account	The select committees are increasingly significant. Ministers must still face questioning in both houses.	MPs still lack expertise, knowledge, research back-up and time to investigate government thoroughly. Prime Minister's Question Time remains a media 'event' rather than a serious session.
Providing democratic legitimacy	The UK's system is stable, with widespread consent. Parliament provides strong legitimacy.	The House of Lords cannot provide this as it is neither elected nor accountable.
Scrutinising legislation	The House of Lords does an increasingly effective job, often improving legislation and blocking unfair or discriminatory aspects of proposals. Experts in various fields in the Lords use their knowledge to good effect.	As legislative committees in the Commons are whipped, their scrutinising function is largely ineffective.
Controlling government power	Increasingly, both houses are checking the power of government, especially when the governing party does not have a commanding majority in the Commons.	The power of prime ministerial patronage and control by party whips still mean that many MPs are unwilling to challenge government.
Representing constituents	This is an acknowledged strength of the Westminster system.	It is absent in the House of Lords. MPs' care of their constituencies varies from MP to MP. There is still no effective mechanism for removing poorly performing MPs.
Representing outside interests	This is especially strong in the House of Lords. Many MPs, too, support external causes and groups.	When there is a clash between party policy and the interests of groups and causes, party loyalty often wins out.
Representing the national interest	When there is a free vote, both houses are seen at their best. MPs and peers take this very seriously.	When votes are whipped, party loyalty often wins out over national interest.
Acting as a recruiting ground for potential ministers	Parliament is a good training ground for future ministers, demonstrating their abilities well.	Being effective in parliamentary work does not necessarily mean a politician could manage a department of state.

The reform of Parliament

REVISED

The House of Commons

There is little enthusiasm for reform of the House of Commons in the future. However, a number of proposals have been presented or are actually planned. Among them are these:

- The size of the Commons is being reduced, probably to 600 members.
- There have been calls for the departmental select committees to have the power to scrutinise legislation before it is debated in the chamber.
- Many MPs would like to see more opportunities to examine secondary (detailed) legislation.
- The key potential reform would be a change in the electoral system to one which is more proportional. This would usually mean that the government would not win an overall majority, so MPs would be considerably more independent. In other words, the balance of power between the legislature and the executive would shift towards Parliament. This is an example of an **external** reform.

The House of Lords

Table 6.3 summarises arguments concerning possible reform of the Lords.

Table 6.3 Arguments for a reformed second chamber

All-appointed	All-elected	Part elected–part appointed
People with special experience and expertise could be recruited into the legislative process.	An elected second chamber would be wholly democratic.	Such a second chamber could enjoy the advantages of both alternatives. It would increase its legitimacy but retain the services of expert-appointed peers.
The political make-up of an appointed body could be manipulated to act as a counterbalance to the government's House of Commons majority.	If elected by some kind of proportional representation, it would prevent a government having too much power.	It may be that such a compromise is the only one acceptable to MPs and peers of all parties.
Without the need to seek re-election, members would be more independently minded.	Under PR, smaller parties and independent members would gain representation they cannot win through first-past-the-post in the House of Commons.	
It would avoid the possibility of the same party controlling both houses.	Members of the second chamber would be properly accountable.	

The nature of parliamentary bills

Table 6.4 shows the types of legislation that pass through Parliament, with their descriptions.

Table 6.4 Types of legislation

Type of legislation	Description
Public bills	These are bills presented by the government. They are expected to pass successfully into law.
Primary legislation	These are major pieces of legislation either changing the law or granting powers to subsidiary bodies and individuals to make secondary legislation.
Secondary legislation (also called delegated legislation)	These are usually described as ministerial orders. Under powers granted in primary legislation, ministers or other bodies may make minor regulations. Most such orders are not debated in Parliament, but Parliament has the option of vetoing such legislation.
Private members' bills	MPs may enter a ballot allowing five of them each year to present their own proposed piece of legislation. These rarely pass into law unless they receive the support of government. There is usually not enough parliamentary time to consider them.
Private bills	Such bills are presented by individuals or organisations outside government and Parliament. They apply to Parliament for permission to take certain actions (often building or changing land use) which are currently forbidden. They go through a slightly simplified form of parliamentary procedure and are rarely refused.

The legislative process — House of Commons

The key stages in processing a **bill** into law are as follows:

- **First reading:** MPs are informed about the bill or proposed legislation but it is not debated at this stage. Several weeks normally elapse before further progress.
- **Second reading:** the main debate on the bill. If it is passed, it will move to detailed scrutiny.
- **Committee stage:** the bill committee considers the bill line by line and may propose amendments.
- **Report stage:** the bill is debated again, with all the passed amendments included.
- **Third reading:** a final debate and a last opportunity to block the legislation.
- **Passage to other house:** most bills are first presented in the House of Commons, so they next pass to the House of Lords (though it can be the other way round).
- **Same procedures:** except that the Lords scrutinises with a committee of the whole house.
- **Royal assent:** this signifies the formal passage of the bill into law.

> **Bill** A proposal presented to Parliament for legislation. Once passed in Parliament, a bill becomes an Act of Parliament.

The legislative process — House of Lords and the Salisbury Convention

REVISED

The following are features of legislation in the House of Lords:
- The House of Lords is subject to the 1911 and 1949 Parliament Acts.
- These Acts mean the Lords can only delay the passage of legislation for one year.
- The 1911 Act also means the Lords has no legislative control over financial matters.
- The House of Lords is subject to an unwritten constitutional convention — the Salisbury Convention.
- The Salisbury Convention, dating back to the 1940s, means that the Lords cannot obstruct any proposed legislation that was contained in the governing party's last election campaign.
- The legislative procedure of the House of Lords is the same as in the House of Commons, with one main exception.
- The exception is that in the 'committee stage' in the Lords, all peers are entitled to attend and vote. In the Commons, this is done by a committee of nominated MPs.

The role and significance of backbench MPs

REVISED

The main roles played by MPs in the House of Commons are:
- taking part in debates on legislation and voting in divisions
- speaking in general debates on government business
- speaking in backbench debates when national or constituency interests can be aired
- scrutinising proposed legislation at committee stage
- possibly being a member of a House of Commons select committee
- active membership of a campaign committee of MPs on a particular issue
- taking part in fact-finding missions, usually with groups of MPs and often abroad
- membership of a committee formed by their own party to develop policy on a particular issue
- campaigning, lobbying and speaking on behalf of an outside interest or cause
- listening to grievances of constituents against a public body and sometimes acting to try to redress those grievances, including lobbying ministers and government officials
- attending important events in the constituency, including listening to and perhaps joining local campaign groups.

MPs suffer from the following weaknesses in relation to government:
- They are expected to be loyal to the party line as they were elected on the basis of the party's manifesto.
- The government normally enjoys majority support in the House of Commons, which means that few votes in the House are in doubt. However, this does depend on whether the government has a decisive parliamentary majority. This has not been the case since 2010.
- MPs lack research facilities.
- MPs have to divide their time between work in the House and work in their constituencies.
- There are few opportunities for MPs to raise issues on the floor of the House or in committee.

MPs enjoy the following strengths in relation to government:
- They can be influential in select committees.
- Collectively, MPs could thwart the government, so their opinions do have to be considered.
- Determined groups of dissident MPs in the governing party can cause problems for ministers by threatening to obstruct legislation.
- On important parliamentary occasions, MPs can attract considerable public and media attention.
- When the government lacks a decisive majority in the Commons, or any majority at all, small groups of MPs can become extremely influential as they can threaten the government's very survival.

> **Revision activity**
>
> Revise good examples of the work of MPs. Include work:
> 1 In relation to their constituencies.
> 2 In committees.
> 3 In relation to government.

Now test yourself

TESTED

3 Explain the meaning of the following terms relating to the UK Parliament:
- Scrutiny
- Supply days
- Vote of no confidence
- Committee stage
- Second reading

Answers on p. 126

The work and importance of select committees

REVISED

The most important **select committees** sit in the House of Commons. Of these, the two types you should mainly consider are the Public Accounts Committee (PAC) and the departmental select committees, of which there are usually 19, though this may vary depending on how many government departments exist.

> **Select committee** A permanent committee of backbench MPs which has a specific task, mainly to call government to account, but other select committees have different parliamentary roles.

The Public Accounts Committee (PAC)

Possibly the most important select committee, the PAC's characteristics are as follows:
- It scrutinises value for money — the economy, efficiency and effectiveness — of public spending and generally holds the government and its civil servants to account for the delivery of public services.
- Its chair is always a member of the main opposition party.
- The chair has great prestige, not to mention a greater salary than other MPs.
- The chair and members are elected by all MPs and so are not controlled by party leaders.
- Its members, despite being party supporters, always tend to act independently, on the whole ignoring their party allegiance. This means the government has no advantage on the committee, even though it has a majority of members on the committee.
- Its reports are often unanimous in their conclusions, so it stands above party politics.
- It has a high profile in the media. Many of its important hearings are broadcast as news items.

Table 6.5 outlines the key investigations that the PAC has undertaken.

Table 6.5 Key PAC investigations

Date	Investigation	Conclusion and action
2016	Into Google's tax affairs	Google's payment of back tax of £130 million for ten years was considered far too low. HMRC should investigate ways of better regulating the tax affairs of multinational companies and making them more transparent.
2015	Into the effectiveness of cancer care by the NHS	Highly critical of variations in cancer treatment in different regions and for different age groups. Criticised low cure rates and increased waiting times for treatment. Publicity prompted the government to review cancer treatment.
2014	Into the financing of fast broadband for poorly served regions	Highly critical of the way in which government financed the programme and of the poor performance of organisations receiving public funds.
2010	Into the BBC's use of public funds	Highly critical of poor value for money and the BBC's lack of accountability. Recommended the government find ways of making the BBC more accountable for how it spends licence payers' money.

Departmental select committees

These committees have the following characteristics:

- There are 19 such committees, each investigating the work of a government department.
- They scrutinise the work of each department in terms of efficiency, effectiveness, fairness and value for money.
- The members are elected by MPs from the whole House.
- The chair, who receives an increased salary, is elected by the committee.
- The number of members varies between 11 and 14.
- The governing party has a majority on each committee.
- The chairs may be from any political party.
- The small parties have a scattering of members.
- Like the PAC, they act largely independently of party allegiance and often produce unanimous reports.
- Also like the PAC, they can call witnesses who may be ministers, civil servants, outside witnesses such as pressure group representatives, or experts.
- Their reports and recommendations are presented to the whole House of Commons and receive considerable publicity.

Table 6.6 outlines some significant reports from departmental select committees.

Table 6.6 Important departmental select committee reports

Date	Committee	Investigation	Conclusion and action
2016	Work and Pensions	Into the collapse of British Home Stores and the loss of much of the employees' pension fund	The company was reported to the Pensions Regulator.
2016	Business, Innovation and Skills	Into alleged bad working practices at Sports Direct	The company was forced to pay compensation to its workers for paying below minimum wage.
2015	Treasury	Into proposals for stricter regulation of the banking sector	Insisted that the government should implement the recommendations of the Parliamentary Commission on Banking Standards. This pushed policy forward on banking regulation.
2014	Defence	Into the circumstances when the UK should make military interventions in world conflicts	Among many recommendations, urged the government to consider legislation about whether Parliament should control major armed interventions.
2012	Home Affairs	Into the Independent Police Complaints Commission's (IPCC) role in the investigation into the 1997 Hillsborough disaster	The IPPC is investigating the Hillsborough disaster following the 2016 inquest.

Other select committees in the House of Commons

The **Liaison Committee** is made up of all the chairs of the departmental select committees. Twice a year this committee questions the prime minister extensively and sometimes quite aggressively over key aspects of government policy.

The **Backbench Business Committee** determines the business of the house for more than 20 days a year. It decides what backbenchers will debate on those days.

Exam tip

You will need to learn a number of examples of the work of the departmental select committees and the Public Accounts Committee. You can use these as evidence of their role and significance.

Typical mistake

Be careful not to confuse select committees with legislative committees. Legislative committees exclusively consider amendments to proposed legislation, while select committees call government to account.

Now test yourself

4 Look at these descriptions of laws, principles and conventions concerning Parliament. In each case, fill in what is being described.

Description	Principle or convention
A rule guaranteeing the rights of MPs to say whatever they wish without fear of prosecution or being sued for defamation.	
The House of Lords must not obstruct proposals which were contained in the governing party's last election manifesto.	
The House of Lords can only delay government legislation for one year.	
A brief opportunity for backbench MPs to raise a special issue on the floor of the House.	

5 Identify three types of committee operating in the House of Commons and one type of committee operating in the House of Lords.

Answers on p. 126

The role and importance of the opposition

The general term **opposition** refers to the following features:
- All MPs and peers who are not members of the governing party may be described as 'opposition MPs and peers'.
- The 'official opposition' is the second largest party in the House of Commons.
- The leader of that party is described as 'leader of the opposition'.
- The leader of the opposition has special privileges, notably to speak in debates and to take the main role at Prime Minister's Questions.
- The leader of the opposition (as well as leaders of other parliamentary parties) takes part in ceremonial state occasions and usually meets visiting dignitaries and heads of state.

The role of the opposition includes:
- forcing the government to explain and justify its policies and decisions
- highlighting the shortcomings of the way the government is running the country
- presenting alternative proposals to those of the government if appropriate
- making itself ready to be an alternative government if the current government is defeated at the next general election.

On **supply days**, of which there are normally more than 20 per year, the opposition may debate any issue it wishes and even hold a vote. In 2009, the opposition defeated the government on the issue of whether Nepalese Gurkha soldiers should have the right of residence in the UK.

Opposition A general term referring to all parties that are not part of the government.

Supply days An historical term nowadays relating to parliamentary days which are under the control of opposition parties rather than the government.

Revision activity

Make sure you thoroughly revise the importance of parliamentary opposition. Look at these areas:
1 Accountability.
2 Debates.
3 Legislation.

Ministerial questions and accountability

The UK Parliament calls ministers to account in a number of ways. These include the following:
- All ministers have to appear before the Commons on a regular basis to answer questions. They may face criticism and will be required to explain and justify policy and decisions.
- Ministers who are peers also have to appear regularly in the Lords.

- Ministers must answer written questions from MPs and peers.
- The prime minister faces Prime Minister's Questions every week, during which they are questioned by the leader of the opposition and backbench MPs.
- The prime minister is also questioned by the Liaison Committee of the House of Commons twice a year.
- During debates on legislation or general policy, ministers must appear in the UK Parliament to justify the government's position.

Now test yourself

TESTED ☐

6 Look at the following forms of action taken in Parliament. In each case, state which kind of body (state whether in the Commons or Lords) carries them out.

Parliamentary activity	Institution which carries it out
Examining the work of government departments	
Delaying legislation for at least one year	
Scrutiny of legislation by the whole House	
Debating great issues largely free of party control	
Examining the effectiveness of the government's financial arrangements	

7 Outline three features of departmental select committees.

Answers on p. 126

Exam practice

AS

1 Describe the main functions of departmental select committees. [10]
2 Describe the main features of the official parliamentary opposition. [10]
3 Using the source, explain how backbench MPs can perform a meaningful political role. [10]

Backbench MPs have been criticised in the past on a number of grounds. The terms 'lobby fodder' and 'party hacks' have been used about them, suggesting that their role is very limited and that they are so much controlled by the party leaders and whips that they lack any independence at all. However, these criticisms may have been exaggerated.

It is too easy to ignore the role of MPs in their own constituencies. Many of them spend a great deal of their time taking up grievances raised by their constituents and all of them hold regular 'surgeries'. MPs also often take up the cause of their constituencies in general. If a government decision or policy might adversely affect the constituency, many of them may break their party allegiance to campaign on behalf of those whom they represent. In recent times, issues such as fracking, airport expansion and the building of onshore wind farms have attracted the attention of hard-working backbenchers.

A sizeable minority also sit on select committees whose role is to call to account ministers and government. This work is extremely influential and MPs acquire a good deal of status from membership. Nevertheless, membership of legislative committees is relatively unimportant as the party whips control the outcome of their deliberations.

Source: original material

In your response you must use knowledge and understanding to analyse points that are only in the source. You will **not** be rewarded for introducing any additional points that are not in the source.

4 'Select committees have now effectively taken over from the official opposition as the main way in which government is called to account in the UK.' How far do you agree with this view of Parliament? [30]

→

A-level

1 Evaluate the extent to which the House of Lords performs a meaningful role in UK democracy. [30]

2 Evaluate the extent to which Parliament is able effectively to call government to account. [30]

3 Using the source, evaluate the respective claims of the two Houses of Parliament to be truly representative institutions. [30]

It is often suggested that the reason the House of Commons has more status than the House of Lords is because it is genuinely representative while the House of Lords is certainly not. This is really for just one overwhelming reason: the Commons is elected but the Lords is not. If we look more deeply, however, the assertion can be challenged.

The electoral system used for general elections ensures that the representation of parties in the Commons is disproportionate. The parties with concentrated support — Labour, Conservative and Scottish Nationalist — have a disproportionally large representation, while those with dispersed support, such as UKIP and the Liberal Democrats, are heavily under-represented. It is also true that the House of Commons contains too few women (about a quarter) and too few members of ethnic minorities in relation to the whole population. Minorities find it difficult to gain representation in the House of Commons because the party whips maintain such a tight grip on MPs.

The unelected, unaccountable House of Lords seems, at first sight, to be remarkably undemocratic. However, it is undeniably true that the representation of parties in the Lords is more accurate than it is in the Commons, with a large group of Liberal Democrats present and some representation for small parties. The social make-up of the Lords is similar to that of the Commons, too. But it is in the representation of minority interests that the Lords can claim superiority. In debates and when scrutinising legislation, the much more independent members of the House of Lords are very willing to put forward the interests of minorities to a much greater degree than MPs in the Commons. Many peers have special expertise and experience, qualities that make them uniquely qualified to represent such minorities.

Source: original material

In your response you must:
- compare the different opinions in the source
- consider this view and the alternative to this view in a balanced way
- use knowledge and understanding to help you analyse and evaluate.

Answers and quick quiz 6 online

ONLINE

Summary

You should now have an understanding of:
- the distinction between the nature, role and importance of the House of Commons and the House of Lords
- the work of MPs and peers
- the extent to which the two Houses of Parliament can call government to account
- the work of both select and legislative committees
- the effectiveness of opposition in Parliament
- the effectiveness of backbenchers in the Commons and peers in the Lords
- questions to ministers and Prime Minister's Question Time — you will be required to describe and evaluate this topic.

7 The prime minister and executive

The structure of the executive

The structure of the UK executive has the following elements:
- The prime minister and her or his close advisers.
- The cabinet: 20–25 senior ministers appointed by the prime minister.
- Various bodies that feed information and advice into the cabinet and to the prime minister.
- Government departments: of these, the Treasury holds a place of special importance as it controls government finances. Many heads of these departments are members of the cabinet. Others may not be in cabinet but are nonetheless influential.
- The senior civil servants who serve government ministers: of these, the cabinet secretary is the most senior. He or she serves both the prime minister personally and the cabinet collectively.
- Various advisers and policy-developing bodies (often called **think tanks**) that serve government departments.
- There may also be a few very senior officials of the governing party who hold no official post but who are intimately involved in policy development.

> **Think tank** An organisation outside government (though sometimes originally set up by government) that carries out research and recommends policy options. Think tanks are staffed by experts, academics and former politicians or civil servants and funded by organisations such as universities, businesses, trade unions, professional associations or government.

The prime minister

The position of UK prime minister can best be understood in terms of the following features of the office:
- The official title of the prime minister is 'First Lord of the Treasury'. Although this is an honorary title, it does indicate that the prime minister has ultimate control over economic policy.
- He or she is the leader of the governing party and so commands a majority in the House of Commons.
- He or she enjoys prerogative powers (the **royal prerogative**). These are the powers formerly given to the monarch. As the monarch cannot exercise these powers in a modern democracy, they are exercised instead by the prime minister.
- The prime minister is party leader in the House of Commons. This gives them a degree of control over parliamentary business.
- He or she can claim some authority from the people as a result of winning the previous general election.
- The prime minister is chair of the cabinet and is able to dominate its proceedings.

> **Royal prerogative** A constitutional principle that allows the prime minister to adopt the arbitrary powers which remain to the monarch. They include such powers as patronage, being commander-in-chief and negotiating foreign treaties.
>
> **Cabinet secretary** The most senior civil servant in the UK. The cabinet secretary serves the prime minister and then the cabinet. He or she also organises the work of cabinet and of government at the centre of power.

The prime minister is assisted and supported by a large collection of bodies and individuals. The main examples are as follows:
- The **cabinet secretary**, the head of the whole civil service, is a personal adviser to the prime minister, assisting him or her to manage policy formulation (but not involved directly in policy formulation).
- The prime minister's private office is staffed by senior civil servants who help the prime minister to handle government business.

- The chief of staff is the prime minister's closest aide, helping her or him to secure support for their policies among colleagues.
- The Cabinet Office is a **government department**. It gives policy advice to the prime minister and cabinet. It is staffed by senior civil servants.
- The Number 10 Policy Unit is a group of advisers, not civil servants, who advise the prime minister on various aspects of government policy.
- Special advisers are hired to advise the prime minister on aspects of policy, media relations and political tactics.

> **Government department**
> The business of government is divided into up to 20 departments. These manage policy and its implementation in the key areas of government responsibility such as the Treasury, education and foreign affairs.

The cabinet

REVISED

The following are the main features of the UK cabinet:
- All its members are appointed by the prime minister.
- The prime minister chairs all its meetings unless he or she is indisposed.
- It normally numbers 20–25 members.
- The members are senior government ministers and a few key officials who run the government's business.
- A few senior party figures may not be cabinet members but still attend meetings. The chief government whip is the best example.
- The cabinet normally meets once a week.
- Its proceedings are secret.
- The cabinet secretary, the UK's most senior civil servant, handles the administration of the cabinet, attends all meetings and advises the prime minister on cabinet business.
- Much of the detailed work of cabinet is conducted in **cabinet committees**.
- Cabinet committees are small groups of ministers, chaired by the prime minister or another senior cabinet member.
- Cabinet committees develop policy details and present proposals for the approval of the whole cabinet.
- There is a subcommittee of cabinet known as COBRA (Cabinet Office Briefing Room A), which meets occasionally when there is a major crisis or emergency.

> **Cabinet committee** A subcommittee of the cabinet containing a small group of cabinet and some junior ministers. The committee discusses the details of policy and then presents proposals for the approval of the whole cabinet. Much of the government's work is done in such committees.

> **Typical mistake**
> Students often suggest that the cabinet is a 'policy-making body'. This is misleading. Very occasionally the cabinet, acting collectively, will develop a government policy, but in the vast majority of cases policy is made elsewhere and the cabinet meets merely to ratify those policies.

> **Exam tip**
> The terms 'government' and 'executive' are generally interchangeable, but it is good practice to use the term 'government' when referring to elected ministers and to reserve the use of 'executive' to when you are discussing the wider government, including political advisers and senior civil servants.

Ministers and their departments

REVISED

Most **ministers** (but not all, as some handle the governing party's business) run one of the departments of state. Ministers are ranked into senior and junior posts:
- **Secretary of state:** a senior minister who runs a large department and is most likely also to be a cabinet member.
- **Minister of state:** he or she will run a subdivision of the department and will not be a cabinet minister.

> **Minister** An MP or peer who is promoted by the prime minister either to run a government department or to carry out a specific role for the government or the governing party.

- **Parliamentary under-secretary of state:** a very junior minister who runs a specialised section of the department.
- **Parliamentary private secretary:** an unpaid MP who acts as a link between ministers and MPs. This is the first rung on the ministerial ladder.

There are additional features of ministerial posts:

- Secretaries of state are known as the 'Right Honourable'. This means they are also members of the Privy Council. The Privy Council was originally the private council to the monarch. Today it meets only to discuss matters of internal government business and national security.
- All ministers described above are subject to **collective ministerial responsibility** (see page 98).
- Collectively they are known as the government 'front bench'
- Ministers are served by a section of the civil service and by personal advisers and committees paid for from government funds.

The roles of ministers and their departments are generally to:

- develop policies in their area of responsibility
- prepare the case for the implementation of policy to the cabinet as a whole
- develop a budget, detailing how the funds made available to the department should be allocated
- draft legislation when it is needed
- organise the passage of legislation through Parliament and to speak in debates on the legislation. This includes developing **secondary (or delegated) legislation**
- organise the provision of services under their responsibility
- appear regularly in Parliament and before select committees to answer questions and generally make themselves accountable to Parliament
- make key decisions which do not require cabinet or parliamentary approval
- appear before the media or write articles in newspapers and journals explaining the policies for which they are responsible.

Less than key decisions are made by civil servants and 'signed off' by ministers.

> **Secondary (delegated) legislation** Much of the business of government is conducted using secondary or delegated legislation. These are orders made by ministers which require relatively little parliamentary control.

Roles of the executive in general

REVISED

The UK executive has the following roles:

- the development of government policy
- conducting foreign policy, including relations with other states and international bodies
- organising the country's defence against external and internal threats
- managing the state's finances
- responding to major problems or crises, such as armed conflict, security threats, economic difficulties or social disorder
- controlling and managing the forces of law and order, including the police, courts, armed forces and intelligence services
- drafting and securing the passage of legislation
- organising the implementation of legislation
- organising and managing the services provided by the state.

Table 7.1 summarises the nature and roles of the UK executive.

Table 7.1 The UK's core executive

Element	Roles	Supporting bodies and individuals
The prime minister	Chief policy maker and chief executive. In particular he or she is chief economic policy maker. Head of the governing party.	• Cabinet • Cabinet secretary • Private office of civil servants • Policy unit
Cabinet	Approving policy and settling disputes within government. Determining the government's reaction to crises and emergencies. Determining the presentation of government policy.	• Cabinet committees • Cabinet Office • Cabinet secretary
Treasury	Managing the government's finances. Determining the quantity and distribution of taxation in the country.	• Senior civil servants • Special advisers • Think tanks
Government departments	Developing and implementing specialised policies. Responsibility for various aspects of the government's roles.	• Civil servants • Special advisers • Think tanks

Typical mistake

Don't confuse the position of ministers with that of civil servants and political advisers. The latter two are not elected and not accountable. They are therefore not subject to prime ministerial patronage. Advisers can lose their jobs for political reasons, while civil servants cannot.

Proposing budgets and legislation

REVISED

A large part of the work of the UK executive is taken up with the government's budget and with drafting and processing legislation. The budget requires the following activities:

- The Treasury prepares an **annual budget** showing how public funds will be allocated to various departments.
- The allocation of funds is negotiated between the Treasury and individual department ministers.
- The final allocation of funds has to be approved in the cabinet.
- The Treasury makes plans to raise the necessary revenue to pay for government services. This is made up mostly of taxes, borrowing and the sale of assets.
- The types and levels of taxation are generally determined by the chancellor of the exchequer in consultation with the prime minister.

Annual budget The government's plans for the annual levels of spending and the taxes to be levied. It also determines whether the government will be borrowing money or achieving a surplus.

- Total expenditure and total revenue plans are made by the Treasury.
- The government's annual budgetary plans have to be approved by the House of Commons.
- The House of Commons will never reject the whole of the government's budget as this would bring government to a halt. However, occasionally the House of Commons may insist on amending details of taxation and spending, including the level and administration of welfare benefits.

Legislation requires the following arrangements:

- Consultation papers (Green Papers and **White Papers**) are drawn up by civil servants in advance of legislation (normally a year), so that MPs, peers and interested parties can make comments and suggest changes.
- Specialised civil servants draft legislation in consultation with ministers and other civil servants.
- The governing party's business managers (leaders of the Houses of Commons and Lords) arrange for parliamentary time to be available for the legislative process. This is done in consultation with the Speaker of each house.
- The business managers and cabinet arrange for speakers to explain and support the legislation in Parliament.
- The party whips check that there is sufficient support for legislation among the governing party's MPs.

> **White Paper** A document outlining the details of a proposed piece of legislation. It is usually published about a year before the legislation is presented to Parliament. Parliament will normally debate the White Paper and proposed changes may be considered.

Individual ministerial responsibility

REVISED

Individual ministerial responsibility is a constitutional convention. It has four main elements:

1 Ministers must be prepared to be accountable to Parliament for the policies and decisions made by their department. This means answering questions in the House, facing interrogation by select committees and justifying their actions in debate.
2 If a minister makes a serious error of judgement, he or she should be required to resign.
3 If the minister's department makes a serious error, whether or not the minister was involved in the cause of the error, he or she is honour-bound to resign.
4 If a minister's conduct falls below the standards required of someone in public office, he or she should leave office and may face dismissal by the prime minister.

However, there has been considerable erosion of the principle. In particular, certain developments have undermined it:

- Ministers are no longer prepared to accept responsibility for errors or poor performance by their departments. Unless a major error can be directly attributed to the minister and is very serious, ministers do not normally resign.
- This means that ministers are prepared to lay the blame on lower-ranking officials and civil servants. In the past, such unelected officials were protected by the doctrine of individual ministerial responsibility.
- It is now up to the prime minister to decide whether a minister should be removed from office under the doctrine.

Collective ministerial responsibility

Collective ministerial responsibility is an unwritten convention of the constitution. The principles of this constitutional convention are as follows:

1 Ministers are collectively responsible for all government policies, even though it may appear that decisions are made by the prime minister or another minister individually.
2 It is based on the principle that government is collegial or collective in nature. The government stands or falls collectively on the basis of its policies.
3 All ministers must publicly support all government policies, even if they disagree with them privately.
4 If a minister wishes to dissent publicly from a government policy, he or she is expected to resign first.
5 If a minister dissents without resigning, he or she can expect to be dismissed by the prime minister.
6 As cabinet meetings are secret, any dissent within government is concealed. This ensures that ministers will not be inhibited in expressing reservations about policies.

Table 7.2 describes several important resignations under the doctrine.

Table 7.2 Examples of collective ministerial responsibility operating

Minister	Position	Party	Resignation year	Reason for resignation
Robin Cook	Foreign secretary	Labour	2003	Opposed the government's decision to take part in an invasion of Iraq.
Clare Short	Overseas development secretary	Labour	2003	Disagreed with UK policy in Iraq.
Iain Duncan Smith	Work and pensions secretary	Conservative	2016	Disagreed with proposed cuts in disability benefits.
Baroness Warsi	Junior foreign office minister	Conservative	2016	Disagreed with the government's policy on Israel and Palestine.
Lord O'Neill	Junior Treasury minister	Conservative	2016	Disagreed with government policy on nuclear power station financing.

Collective ministerial responsibility is important for the following reasons:
● It gives the government a strong sense of unity.
● It can help the prime minister maintain his or her dominant position.
● It stifles dissidence within the government.
● It helps ministers express their reservations privately.
● It can protect individual ministers from pressure if the government takes collective responsibility for a policy.

Exam tip

When discussing the doctrine of collective responsibility, it is crucial to quote at least two prominent examples of ministerial resignations.

Typical mistake

Some students believe that collective responsibility extends only to members of the cabinet. This is not the case: collective responsibility applies to all government ministers and ministerial aides.

The powers of the prime minister

These are the prime minister's main powers:

- Powers which can be described as prerogative powers and are therefore permanent and available to all prime ministers, no matter what their short-term circumstances:
  - Prime ministers have complete power to appoint or dismiss all government ministers (known as **patronage**), whether in the cabinet or outside the cabinet. They also have a say in other public appointments, including the most senior civil servants.
  - They have power to negotiate foreign treaties, including trade arrangements with other states or international organisations.
  - The prime minister is commander-in-chief of the armed forces and can commit them to action. However, it should be noted that this power has come under challenge in recent times. It is now accepted that the prime minister should make major military commitments only 'on the advice and with the sanction of Parliament'. Nevertheless, once armed forces have been committed to action, the prime minister has general control of their actions.
  - The prime minister conducts foreign policy and determines relationships with foreign powers. In this sense he or she represents the country internationally.
  - Prime ministers head the cabinet system (see below), choose its members, set its agenda and determine what cabinet committees should exist and who should sit on them.
- Powers which are not prerogative powers but which prime ministers are expected to exercise:
  - The prime minister is chief policy maker. This power derives from their being the governing party leader.
  - It is generally true that the prime minister sets the tone of economic policy. Normally this is done alongside the chancellor of the exchequer, who is normally a close colleague.
  - The prime minister can speak for the country when abroad or meeting other heads of state.

> **Patronage** The power of appointment and dismissal. In relation to the prime minister, patronage over ministerial offices gives them great power because it promotes loyalty among those who are promoted or who hope to be promoted.

> **Typical mistake**
>
> Under the royal prerogative the prime minister is 'commander-in-chief'. This does not mean that he or she literally commands the armed forces — this is done by senior military figures. What it does mean is that the prime minister has the ultimate say in whether UK forces will be deployed and determines the limitations on their actions.

> **Typical mistake**
>
> There is some confusion over whether the royal prerogative applies to the prime minister alone or to the government as a whole. The reality is that it applies to both. It is important because when prerogative powers are being exercised, they may be used in the name of the government, but ultimately they require the full support of the prime minister.

> **Revision activity**
>
> Make sure you thoroughly revise the importance of these three features of executive government:
> 1 Patronage.
> 2 Collective responsibility.
> 3 Prerogative powers.

The powers of the cabinet

We should place the prime minister and cabinet together when discussing power at the centre of government. Between them they control government and direct the political agenda. They have the following powers:

- They determine government policy.
- They establish the presentation of that policy.
- They control Parliament's agenda.
- They determine government priorities, establishing a programme of action.

- Whatever the cabinet declares is policy is binding on the party. This does not guarantee compliance, but it carries a great deal of authority.
- Between them they direct foreign policy.
- Between them they direct economic and financial policy.
- They determine the government's reaction to crises and emergencies.
- They direct any military action taking place abroad.

The selection of ministers

REVISED

The qualities required to be a government minister include:
- loyalty — this is a key quality; prime ministers are reluctant to promote dissidents who challenge the party line
- ability to handle difficult situations in Parliament — ministers are constantly being called to account on the floor of the House and in select committees
- ability to handle the media
- potential ability to manage a large department with many officials and a large budget
- popularity within the governing party.

When constructing an effective cabinet, the prime minister may take these considerations into account:
- Many prime ministers prefer a cabinet that is ideologically unified. This was certainly the case with Tony Blair (1997–2007) and Margaret Thatcher (1979–90).
- Some prime ministers prefer or are forced into constructing a balanced cabinet with representatives from different parts of the party. This was done by John Major (1990–97) and David Cameron (2010–16).
- Increasingly, prime ministers are concerned with the social balance of the cabinet, so they promote a good number of women and members of ethnic minorities.
- One or two ministers should be from the House of Lords so that there is senior government representation in that house.

The relationship between the prime minister and the cabinet

REVISED

The prime minister can control the cabinet in a number of ways:
- Patronage is a key element. Because the prime minister solely appoints and dismisses ministers, all members of the cabinet owe the prime minister their loyalty. The threat of dismissal is a powerful weapon to use against dissident ministers. All prime ministers use patronage to control cabinet and dismiss and appoint ministers routinely to maintain loyalty. Theresa May cleared out a large minority of David Cameron's former Conservative cabinet in 2016 to ensure cabinet unity.
- Some prime ministers use patronage to fill the cabinet with their close supporters — examples are Margaret Thatcher and Tony Blair. This means the prime minister can always rely upon a majority of support in cabinet.
- Another key element is **collective responsibility** (see pages 97–98). This convention says that all members of the government must defend government policy, even if they disagree privately. If a minister speaks out against government policy, he or she must resign.

- By convention, the prime minister controls the cabinet agenda. By determining what cabinet will discuss, he or she can avoid opposition and conflict and show preference for their own policies.
- The prime minister is closely assisted by the most influential senior civil servant, the cabinet secretary. The cabinet secretary has influence over all government departments, so helps to secure prime ministerial control.
- The prime minister makes appointments to cabinet committees (see above) which discuss and propose policy detail. By manipulating the membership of these committees, the prime minister can exert control.
- Most prime ministers maintain an 'inner cabinet' of close, senior ministerial colleagues who have great influence of their own. They can control cabinet by reaching separate agreements within the inner cabinet.
- Some prime ministers prefer to reach agreements with colleagues outside cabinet and then present the others with a *fait accompli* at formal meetings. Under Tony Blair this became known as **sofa politics**.

> **Sofa politics** A term made popular under Tony Blair. It referred to his practice of holding informal meetings (on the 'sofa' at Downing Street) with powerful ministers in order to settle policies outside the cabinet itself.

Exam tip

Students are often unsure how far to go back historically when discussing the experience of prime ministers. In general, you should seek to use examples which are as recent as possible. However, if the only example you can use is from much further back in time, it is better to use it than to use no example at all. Certainly, evidence since 1979 (Margaret Thatcher) is perfectly valid.

Table 7.3 details the relative powers of the prime minister and the cabinet.

Table 7.3 Prime minister–cabinet relations

The powers of the prime minister	The powers of the cabinet
The prime minister is perceived by the public to be government leader and representative of the nation. This gives them great authority.	If the cabinet is determined, a majority of members can overrule the prime minister.
Prime ministerial patronage means the prime minister has power over ministers and can demand loyalty.	Ultimately the cabinet can effectively remove the prime minister from office, as happened to Margaret Thatcher (1990) and Tony Blair (2007).
The prime minister now has a wide range of individuals or bodies that advise them personally.	Cabinet may control powerful ministers with a large following who can thwart the will of the prime minister. Tony Blair was rivalled by Gordon Brown in 2005–07, David Cameron by several influential Eurosceptics in 2010–15.
The prime minister chairs the cabinet and controls its agenda, which means he or she can control the governing process. The prime minister enjoys prerogative powers and so can bypass cabinet on some issues.	If the prime minister leads a divided party, it is more difficult to control cabinet. This happened to John Major in 1992–97 and was a constant problem for David Cameron.
The prime minister can use collective responsibility to silence critics and hold cabinet together.	Ministers can 'leak' disagreements to the media and to colleagues, and so undermine the prime minister by publicising cabinet splits.

Now test yourself

1 The table shows the prime minister's powers. In the right-hand column add a brief description of the limits to these powers.

Power	Limitations
To appoint or dismiss ministers	
To conduct foreign policy	
To control cabinet	
To make government policy	
To call a general election	

2 Explain the differences between individual and collective ministerial responsibility.

Answers on pp. 126–27

Revision activity

Make sure you thoroughly revise the role of the following:
1 Cabinet.
2 Cabinet committees.
3 The cabinet secretary.

How powerful is the prime minister?

REVISED

Although we think of prime ministers as all-powerful, there are long-term and short-term limitations on their authority and power. Table 7.4 summarises these.

Table 7.4 The limitations on the power of the prime minister

Prime ministerial limitations	Adverse circumstances for a prime minister	Examples
The prime minister may be overruled by the cabinet.	If the cabinet is split or if the prime minister tries to impose a controversial policy.	Margaret Thatcher in 1990 when she tried to impose the controversial poll tax
The prime minister may not be able to command Parliament.	He or she may have a slim parliamentary majority or lose the majority altogether.	John Major, 1992–97 David Cameron, 2010–16
Adverse events may render the prime minister relatively powerless.	Economic crises can cause major problems for a prime minister.	Gordon Brown, 2008–10
The prime minister may lose the confidence of their own party.	A split in the party can undermine the prime minister.	Tony Blair, 2005–07
Though the prime minister has wide patronage powers, he or she may be forced to appoint to the cabinet adversaries who have a strong following in the party.	There is a dissident wing in the governing party which may be held in check if some of its members are promoted to cabinet.	John Major, 1990–97 David Cameron, 2010–15

Some commentators have described the prime minister as effectively a president, leading **presidential government**. Table 7.5 expresses this argument.

Table 7.5 Is the prime minister effectively a president?

Yes	No
The prime minister takes on many of the roles of head of state and speaks for the nation.	He or she is not head of state.
The election of the governing party owes much to the prime minister's leadership.	The prime minister is not directly elected.
Despite parliamentary constraints the prime minister is chief foreign policy maker.	The prime minister's conduct of foreign policy is increasingly subject to parliamentary approval.
Once in action the prime minister makes strategic military decisions.	The prime minister can no longer commit armed forces to action without parliamentary approval.
The prime minister controls the intelligence services at home and abroad.	A prime minister can be removed from office by Parliament or by their own party while a president cannot.
The prime minister negotiates and agrees foreign treaties.	The powers of the prime minister are not codified in a constitution but are conventional.
Some charismatic prime ministers such as Churchill, Thatcher and Blair have adopted a presidential 'style'.	Prime ministers cannot promote patriotic support for the state to the same extent as presidents often do.

> **Presidential government**
> A name given to the power of the prime minister suggesting that he or she is as much like an American president as a UK head of state.

> **Exam tip**
> It is vital, when discussing the office of prime minister, that you deploy evidence about the experience of at least two past prime ministers.

Now test yourself

TESTED

3 Look at the following descriptions. What or who is being described in each case?

Description	What is being described
The doctrine that a government minister should resign if their department makes a serious mistake	
A convention that allows the prime minister to exercise the arbitrary powers of the monarch	
The power of the prime minister that derives from their power over ministerial appointments and dismissals	
A subdivision of the cabinet where many policies are worked out in detail	
The civil servant who helps the prime minister to manage the cabinet	

4 Outline three prerogative powers enjoyed by the prime minister.

Answers on p. 127

How powerful is the cabinet?

REVISED

The cabinet has a number of permanent powers:

- It has the ultimate power to make government decisions legitimate within the governing party.
- It can overrule the prime minister on policy if there is a 'critical mass' willing to make a stand.
- It makes key decisions if the prime minister refers an issue to it.
- It has control over the government's parliamentary business.

The cabinet's power within government depends on varying circumstances:

- how secure the prime minister is within their own party
- how dominant the prime minister is
- how secure the government is within Parliament
- whether the governing party is united or divided.

Table 7.6 considers both cabinet and prime ministerial government.

Table 7.6 Cabinet government or prime ministerial government?

Cabinet government	Prime ministerial government
All domestic government policy has to be legitimised by the cabinet.	The prime minister dominates the political system.
A concerted cabinet can overrule the prime minister.	The prime minister has extensive prerogative powers.
Detailed consideration of government policy takes place in cabinet committees.	The prime minister dominates foreign policy.
The prime minister cannot risk a cabinet revolt and so must consult colleagues regularly.	Collective responsibility gives the prime minister great authority.
	Prime ministerial patronage commands loyalty.

Prime ministerial profiles

REVISED

The following four profiles can be used as evidence in assessing prime ministerial power. The particular circumstances of each prime minister are described.

Margaret Thatcher

In office: 1979–90

Majorities: 1979: 43, 1983: 144, 1987: 102

Description of political stance: neo-liberal and neo-conservative

Advantages:
- Decisive parliamentary majorities.
- Good image in a high proportion of the press.
- Good public image among the middle classes.
- Reputation for strength in foreign policy.
- Respected by foreign leaders.
- After 1983 led an ideologically united party.
- Hailed a national hero following the success of the war to liberate the Falkland Islands from Argentinian occupation.
- There was an economic boom in the mid-1980s.
- Strongly backed by cabinet after 1983.

Disadvantages:
- Poor public image among the working classes.
- Liberal and left-wing media criticised her heavily.
- Obstinacy in pushing the unpopular poll tax policy led to her downfall.
- In her latter years the economic situation began to deteriorate.
- A small, moderate group in the party opposed her implacably.

Circumstances of her downfall:
Thatcher refused to drop her support for the introduction of an unpopular form of local taxation known as the poll tax. When it was feared that the party would be defeated at the 1992 general election, a leadership challenge was mounted and Thatcher was replaced by John Major in 1990.

Tony Blair

In office: 1997–2007

Majorities: 1997: 179, 2001: 167, 2005: 66

Description of political stance: moderate social democrat (*third way* or *New Labour*)

Advantages:
- Decisive parliamentary majorities.
- Good image in a high proportion of the press up to 2003.
- Charismatic public image among both the working and middle classes until 2003.
- Positive image abroad until the Iraq war in 2003.
- There was an economic boom in the later 1990s.
- Respected by foreign leaders.
- Led an ideologically united party.

Disadvantages:
- Public image became tarnished in later years.
- After 2003 faced strong opposition from the well-supported Gordon Brown.
- The Iraq war proved to be a disaster for his reputation.

Circumstances of his downfall:
Blair's reputation declined after the Iraq war. Increasing numbers of Labour members wanted to see Gordon Brown as their leader. Pressure built up as Brown became more popular. Blair resigned in 2007 in favour of Brown.

David Cameron

In office: 2010–16

Majorities: 2010: no majority, 2015: 12

Description of political stance: liberal, progressive conservative

Advantages:
- Good public and media image.
- Supported by the Liberal Democrats in the coalition government.
- Enjoyed the support of powerful figures in the Conservative Party.
- Opposition Labour Party was weak and increasingly disunited.
- Enjoyed a good reputation abroad.

Disadvantages:
- Forced into coalition government in 2010. This severely reduced his control over government.
- Won only a very narrow parliamentary majority in 2015.
- Constantly faced opposition from right-wing Eurosceptics within his own party.
- Forced to introduce a programme of severe economic austerity.

Circumstances of his downfall:
As a result of pressure from his own party and the rise of UKIP, Cameron was forced to promise a referendum on UK membership of the EU in 2016. When the outcome was to leave the EU after he had campaigned strongly to remain, his reputation was destroyed and he resigned.

Theresa May

In office: 2016–

Majorities: 2016: 12, 2017: no majority

Description of political stance: one nation conservative

Advantages:
- Leads a largely united party.
- Opposition is fragmented.
- Few viable alternatives to her leadership in her party.

Disadvantages:
- Attempting (from June 2017) to govern without a majority. She lacks elective authority and a clear mandate.
- Reputation was damaged by her decision to call a general election in June 2017 with such disastrous results.
- Dependent on the success of Brexit negotiations so her destiny is not in her own hands.
- Relies on the fragile support of the DUP to survive.

Revision activity

Make sure you thoroughly revise examples of the following:
1 A prime minister who lost office by losing an election.
2 A prime minister who was forced to resign by their cabinet.
3 A prime minister who was forced to resign as a result of an event beyond their control.

Now test yourself

TESTED

5 Identify a prime minister and the details which fit the description in the table.

Description	Prime minister	Details
He or she resigned after losing a referendum vote.		
He or she became prime minister without fighting a general election.		
He or she was forced to fight a leadership contest after losing support for a key policy.		
He or she resigned in favour of a rival from within their own party.		
He or she lost a general election after governing for seven years.		

6 Describe the circumstances under which Theresa May became prime minister in 2016.

Answers on p. 127

Exam practice

AS

1 Describe the main functions of the cabinet. [10]
2 Describe the main features of collective ministerial responsibility. [10]
3 Using the source, explain the importance of prime ministerial patronage. [10]

There used to be a principle in British political life that if a minister made a serious error, or if their department made a mistake, the minister was expected to resign their post, *whether or not they were to blame directly for the problem*. In recent times, however, it appears that this principle has fallen into disuse. Ministers are quite happy to push the blame for mistakes downwards to their civil servants and advisers. The reality now is that if a minister has the backing of the prime minister, their position remains secure. Indeed, many more ministers resign because they disagree with government policy than because their department is operating poorly.

All ministers owe their position to the prime minister, who has complete control over ministerial appointments. They have complete power over hiring and firing. This means that all ministers owe a debt of loyalty to the prime minister. Nevertheless, it is important to note that some ministers can be 'too powerful to sack' and some have to be included in the cabinet because they lead an important faction in the governing party, suggesting they would cause too many problems for the government if they were sitting on the backbenches. Patronage and party loyalty are important realities in UK politics, but they cannot always be guaranteed to ensure the unity of government.

Source: original material

In your response you must use knowledge and understanding to analyse points that are only in the source. You will **not** be rewarded for introducing any additional points that are not in the source.
4 'The prime minister is now effectively a president.' How far do you agree with this view of the position of the prime minister? [30]

A-level

1 Evaluate the extent to which the cabinet can shape policy and control the power of the prime minister. [30]

2 Evaluate the extent to which the limitations on the role of the prime minister will ultimately outweigh the powers of the office. [30]

3 Using the source, evaluate the extent to which prime ministers are able to dominate the political system. [30]

The experiences of two former UK prime ministers help us to understand both the strengths and weaknesses of the office which they held.

The first was Tony Blair, who took office in 1997 after winning a landslide victory in the general election. Blair was one of the inspirations behind the New Labour movement that dominated politics for ten years. He led a cohort of politicians, including Gordon Brown, Robin Cook and Peter Mandelson, who shared the same political vision. His government, using its massive parliamentary majority, was able to implement a programme of constitutional reform and to shift large proportions of the state's resources towards health and education provision. Blair and his predecessor, John Smith, had been able to defeat the left wing of the Labour Party and so moved Labour Party politics closer to the centre of the political spectrum. Blair was a dominant politician in other senses of the words, too. He was viewed as charismatic and enjoyed a positive media image, at least until he led the UK into a disastrous conflict in Iraq.

By contrast, his successor Gordon Brown, who took over in 2007, was unable to dominate in the same way. Brown was certainly not as charismatic as Blair and although Labour enjoyed a comfortable parliamentary majority after 2005, this was not as decisive as Blair's two three-digit majorities. As time went by, too, it was clear that the Labour Party was now divided between those who continued to support Blair's vision and those who followed Brown's more left-wing ideas and his growing Euroscepticism. But it was perhaps the financial crisis that overwhelmed the Western world in 2008 that did most to derail Brown's premiership. Though the crisis was not of his making, Brown was often blamed for the aftermath, which involved a huge growth in the national debt and a long period of economic austerity.

Brown and Blair did have one feature in common. This was that they lost power largely because of external events — the Iraq war in Blair's case and the financial crisis in Brown's. This may lead us to the conclusion that, however popular or unpopular a prime minister may be in the short term, in the long term their power depends on factors beyond their control.

Source: original material

In your response you must:
- compare the different opinions in the source
- consider this view and the alternative to this view in a balanced way
- use knowledge and understanding to help you analyse and evaluate.

Answers and quick quiz 7 online

ONLINE

Summary

You should now have an understanding of:
- the nature of the executive branch of government
- the powers of the prime minister
- the limitations on prime ministerial power and how to compare them to his or her powers
- the extent to which the prime minister is effectively a president
- the nature, role and powers of the cabinet
- the relationship between the prime minister and the cabinet
- the doctrine of individual ministerial responsibility
- the nature and importance of collective ministerial responsibility
- the experience of at least three prime ministers
- how to use information about at least three prime ministers to illustrate the strengths and weaknesses of the position
- the historical changes in the relationship between the prime minister and the rest of the political system.

8 Relations between branches

The role and composition of the Supreme Court

The membership of the court is as follows:
- There are 12 senior judges.
- All Supreme Court judges have long and extensive experience of sitting on cases from any part of the UK.
- The head of the court is the president of the Supreme Court.
- The judges are appointed by an independent panel of the country's senior legal figures.

The role of the judiciary as a whole is wider than that of the Supreme Court:
- **Dispensing justice:** hearing criminal cases and civil disputes.
- **Making law:** not all law is developed by Parliament, some is made by judges when they interpret the meaning of law and declare what is **common law**. This is done through **judicial precedent**.
- **Interpreting law:** when the meaning and application of law are unclear it is the role of judges to interpret its true meaning.
- **Establishing case law:** judges decide how the law is to be applied in particular kinds of case. Once established, other courts follow the same case law.
- **Declaring common law:** judges sometimes declare what law should be, as we commonly understand it.
- **Judicial review:** courts hear cases brought by citizens, usually against government and the state, when they believe they have been treated unfairly or unequally. Very often these cases apply the terms of the European Convention on Human Rights.
- **Public inquiries:** judges sometimes hold inquiries into matters of major public concern and recommend action to government and Parliament.

The Supreme Court itself has a narrower but more important role than the lower courts:
- It is the final court of appeal for all civil cases in the United Kingdom and criminal cases from England, Wales and Northern Ireland. It may hear **constitutional law** cases, as well as both criminal and **civil law** cases.
- It hears appeals on arguable points of law of general public importance. This means it clarifies the meaning and application of law which may not be clear from the wording of the law.
- It concentrates on cases of the greatest public and constitutional importance.
- It maintains and develops the role of the highest court in the United Kingdom as a leader in the common law world. Essentially this means it is the leading interpreter of common law.

Common law Unwritten law that can be declared by a court on the grounds that certain rules have existed for a long time and are generally accepted by people as law. Common law often concerns the rights that citizens enjoy. Such law is passed down through judicial precedents.

Judicial precedent A legal principle that when a court makes a particular interpretation of the meaning of law or a judgment about how the law should be applied in a specific case, that interpretation must be followed by all courts in subsequent cases. Only a higher court can overturn a judicial precedent.

Judicial review Any citizen or organisation may apply for a review of a decision or regulation made by a public body. This will be conducted by a court presided over by a judge. Typical cases involve discrimination, lack of consultation, lack of fairness or an abuse of human rights.

Constitutional law Laws, which may be written law or common law or conventional rules, which concern the ways in which government operates and the distribution of political power.

Civil law Unlike criminal law, which involves criminal activity, civil law refers to private disputes between individuals and organisations.

Table 8.1 outlines some key cases to illustrate the work of the Supreme Court.

Table 8.1 Important cases in the Supreme Court

Case	Year	Legal or constitutional principle	Issue	Outcome
Miller	2017	On appeal from the High Court. The case concerned the extent of the prerogative powers of government.	Miller, a private citizen, sought a judicial review of the government's refusal to allow the UK Parliament to ratify the decision of the 2016 referendum to leave the European Union.	Miller won the case and the government was forced to allow the UK Parliament to vote on whether the UK should leave the EU.
Schindler v *Duchy of Lancaster*	2016	The right to vote.	Should UK citizens who had lived abroad for more than 15 years be able to vote in the 2016 EU referendum?	The vote was denied to such citizens as they had forfeited their rights by living abroad for so long.
PJS v *News Group Newspapers*	2015	Freedom of speech versus the right to privacy.	An unnamed celebrity sought to prevent newspapers from printing details of his/her private life.	The court decided that the right to privacy was superior to the freedom of the press without justification for publication.
Trump International Golf Club v *Scottish ministers*	2015	*Ultra vires* – whether the Scottish government had overstepped its legal powers.	Trump argued that the government had exceeded its powers in allowing a wind farm to be built near his new golf club.	The Scottish government won the case; it had not exceeded its powers.

The principles of the Supreme Court

REVISED

The key features of the court are as follows:
- It is the highest court in the UK.
- It is totally independent of political pressure.

- Its membership is determined on the basis of legal experience and good judgement rather than any political bias.
- Only the UK Parliament can overturn decisions of the Supreme Court by passing new legislation or amending existing law.

> **Typical mistake**
>
> It is sometimes assumed that the UK Supreme Court can overturn a parliamentary statute. This is not so. It can *recommend* the repeal or amendment of a statute but cannot compel the UK Parliament to comply with its recommendations.

The Supreme Court and the **judiciary** play a key role in protecting human rights by:

- enforcing the European Convention on Human Rights
- enforcing the rule of law
- asserting common law rights
- enforcing **freedom of information** cases.

> **Freedom of information** A right, established by the Freedom of Information Act in 2000, of citizens and organisations to have access to official information held by public bodies. The only exceptions are information that might prejudice national security and private information held about other individuals.
>
> **Judiciary** A general term referring to the whole legal system. In terms of politics, the senior judiciary are those judges and courts that make decisions of wider political significance.

Table 8.2 describes three important rights cases.

Table 8.2 Rights cases in the Supreme Court

Case	Year	Principle	Issue	Outcome
Brewster	2017	Whether cohabiting couples have the same joint pensions rights as married couples	Judicial review under the European Convention	Brewster won the case, establishing equal rights for cohabitants.
Evans v Attorney General	2015	Freedom of information	Should Prince Charles's letters to government on various issues be released and published?	It was ruled that the Freedom of Information Act did apply to the royal family's papers.
R v Metropolitan Commissioner for Police	2011	Privacy under the European Convention	Whether the police can hold the DNA records of people who have not been convicted of a crime	It was ruled a breach of privacy and thousands of DNA records had to be destroyed.

Table 8.3 assesses the strengths and weaknesses of the Supreme Court.

Table 8.3 An assessment of the powers of the Supreme Court

Powers	Weaknesses
The independence of the court is guaranteed in law.	It cannot activate its own cases but must wait for appeals to be lodged.
It can set aside executive actions that contradict the European Convention on Human Rights (ECHR) or the rule of law.	The sovereignty of Parliament means that its judgments can be overturned by parliamentary statute.
It can interpret law and so affect the way it is implemented.	The European Court of Human Rights can hear appeals from the court and overturn the decision, but this is not binding.
It cannot overrule the sovereignty of Parliament but it can declare proposed legislation incompatible with the ECHR, which is influential.	
With the UK leaving the EU its judgments cannot be overturned by a higher court.	

> **Typical mistake**
>
> A serious mistake students often make is to assume that the European Convention on Human Rights, which is also part of UK law, is controlled by the European Union. This is very wrong — it has nothing to do with the EU. It is controlled by a different body called the Council of Europe and will therefore still apply after the UK leaves the EU.

Judicial neutrality

REVISED

The neutrality of the whole judiciary, including the Supreme Court, is a key principle. It implies the following:

- Judges should show no political bias.
- Judges should not show any bias in favour of, or against, any section of society.
- Judges should base their judgments purely on the principles of law and justice and not on the basis of their own prejudices.
- As judges have security of tenure they cannot be dismissed on the basis of their judgments. However, the neutrality of the judiciary can be reinforced by the process of appointment of new judges.

Judicial independence

REVISED

Judicial independence is a key principle of a democracy. It is important for a number of reasons:

- Judges need to be able to enforce the rule of law (equality under the law) without any external pressure.
- Judges hear cases of political importance involving the government itself, so they must not be subject to pressure from government if they are to give a neutral judgment.
- Judges must be able to protect the rights of citizens without fear of retribution if they defy government wishes.
- The judiciary is, in some cases, a key check on executive power.

Judicial independence is upheld in a number of ways:

- Judges are appointed for life, so they cannot be dismissed if the government disagrees with their judgments.
- Judges cannot have their incomes threatened if they make decisions against government wishes.
- Judges are appointed by a commission which is independent of government.
- It is the duty of government to protect judges from external pressure, for example from the media.

The influence of the Supreme Court on government and Parliament

The Supreme Court and the rest of the judiciary have various ways of controlling the power of both the UK Parliament and the government. In doing so they are preventing abuses of power and asserting the rights of citizens against the state. The methods they use include the following:

- The courts enforce the European Convention on Human Rights when interpreting executive actions and in cases of judicial review.
- The courts cannot set aside a piece of parliamentary legislation, but they can declare that a law is incompatible with the European Convention, which puts pressure on government to amend the law accordingly.
- Similarly, the courts impose common law, often when asserting the rights of citizens.
- The courts impose the rule of law, ensuring that all citizens are treated equally. This usually occurs as a result of judicial review.
- In cases of *ultra vires* the courts decide whether a public body has exceeded its legal powers. This is also the case when judges rule that the government has exceeded its constitutional powers.
- Public inquiries by judges can be very persuasive in forcing government to take certain actions.

Table 8.4 shows how and why the Supreme Court and the judiciary come into conflict with government.

Table 8.4 Judiciary–government conflicts

Issue	Detail
Sentencing in criminal cases	The judges wish to have a free hand in determining sentences on a case by case basis. The government, which is responsible for law and order, insists it needs to impose minimum sentences for some crimes, such as possession of weapons.
Rights	The judges have a duty to preserve human rights, but these may hinder the government's attempts to maintain national security, notably over terrorism.
Freedom of expression	While the government seeks to control the spread of religious extremism, by prosecuting extreme preachers, etc., the judges have a duty to preserve freedom of expression.
Freedom of information	The government believes some information should be secret in the national interest, while judges view sympathetically appeals under the Freedom of Information Act.
Judicial review	Judges have become more open to hearing appeals by citizens against public bodies which may have acted unlawfully, beyond their powers, have been negligent or have discriminated against certain people. Government claims too many judicial reviews inhibit its ability to govern, notably over such issues as the introduction of fracking, airport expansion, high-speed railway building and new road systems.

Typical mistake

Devolution does not mean that the elected assemblies of Scotland, Wales and Northern Ireland are not bound by Supreme Court decisions. This is because those elected bodies are not sovereign.

Ultra vires and judicial review

The term **ultra vires** has the following meaning and implications:

- It literally means 'beyond the powers'.
- Its value is to prevent public bodies from acting unlawfully.
- It is a common subject of **judicial review**.
- Citizens and organisations may appeal against a decision by a public body on the grounds that it was acting outside the powers granted to it by law.
- The remedy, if a case is proved, is often the cancellation of the decision and sometimes compensation.
- *Ultra vires* can apply to unwritten common law when a public body acts beyond what is 'commonly agreed' to be its common law powers. Schools and hospitals would be typical examples.

> **Ultra vires** A legal principle where citizens may appeal against a decision or action by a public body on the grounds that the body has exceeded its legal powers.
>
> **Judicial review** A review, undertaken by a court, of a law, regulation or decision made by a public body to determine whether it was fair, properly formulated and within the legal powers of the body concerned.

Revision activity

Revise and remember two court cases which illustrate the following:

1 How the Supreme Court protected human rights in the UK.
2 When a senior court declared an action by government to be *ultra vires*.
3 When a senior court ruled against some kind of discrimination operated by a public body.

Exam tip

It is essential that you can explain a number of key legal cases to illustrate any answers concerning the role and power of the judiciary.

Now test yourself

1 Look at the following descriptions. What or who is being described in each case?

Description	What is being described
The legal principle involved when a public body is accused of acting beyond its statutory powers	
The principle that judges must not be influenced by government when considering legal cases	
The principle that judges should not display any obvious political allegiance	
A legal case which is judging whether an action by a public body was fair, within legal powers, was the result of proper procedures and/or treated citizens equally	
The constitutional principle that all citizens, including government, should be treated equally under the law	

2 Outline three ways in which the Supreme Court controls government power.

Answers on pp. 127–28

The influence and effectiveness of the UK Parliament

This should be revised in conjunction with material in Chapter 5.

Although the common belief is that the executive dominates Parliament in the UK, Westminster does have some sway and there are some circumstances where Parliament exercises control. These include the following:

- Parliament has the reserve power to dismiss a government in a vote of no confidence.
- Parliament also has the reserve power to veto government legislation.
- The House of Lords can delay legislation for a year.
- The Commons can amend legislation.
- The House of Lords can also amend legislation, though its decisions can be reversed in the House of Commons.
- Small groups of dissident MPs on the government side can thwart government proposals.
- If the government enjoys a small parliamentary majority or no majority at all, it is highly vulnerable to rebellions and obstruction.
- The departmental select committees have become increasingly effective in calling government to account.
- Similarly, the Public Accounts Committee has become highly influential.
- When the government allows a free vote, MPs or peers may vote according to their beliefs rather than party allegiance. This occurred, for example, over military intervention in Syria and has been used several times to debate foxhunting.
- Ministers are obliged to present themselves before Parliament regularly to account for their decisions and policies.

> **Typical mistake**
>
> It is an error to assume that the UK Parliament has any real power over law making. Laws are developed by the government. The role of Parliament is to scrutinise legislation and to make laws legitimate. Only rarely does Parliament refuse to pass a law proposed by the government. The government has an elective mandate to legislate its policies and Parliament does not have the authority to deny that mandate.

Executive dominance of the UK Parliament

There are a number of ways in which the executive can control Parliament and a number of structural weaknesses which Parliament has to accept:

- It is often said that the government is an **elective dictatorship**, referring to a belief that the government has so much power in relation to Parliament that it can be described as a dictatorship. Today this view is regarded as something of an exaggeration.
- Usually, though not always, the government enjoys the support of the majority of MPs in the House of Commons. It can expect to win virtually every critical vote.
- The patronage of the prime minister demands the loyalty of most of their party's MPs.

> **Elective dictatorship** An expression first used by Conservative politician Lord Hailsham, in 1976. It refers to the belief that as long as the governing party enjoys a parliamentary majority, it is able to drive through any legislation it wishes.

- The government controls the legislative process and can block most amendments from the floors of the Commons and Lords.
- Collective responsibility means the government presents a united front to Parliament.
- The House of Lords lacks democratic legitimacy.
- The House of Lords can delay but cannot veto legislation.
- The Salisbury Doctrine means that the Lords cannot block legislation for which the government has an electoral mandate.
- Ministers are backed by a huge army of civil servants and advisers while MPs and peers lack such back-up.

The changing relationship between Parliament and the executive

Table 8.5 shows how the relationship between government and Parliament can change according to circumstances.

Table 8.5 The changing relationship between the UK Parliament and the executive

Factors in the growing influence of Parliament	Factors that retain executive power
Since 2010 governments in the UK have lacked a decisive parliamentary majority.	When the government is fragile, its supporters tend to be more disciplined to keep themselves in power.
Parliament is achieving considerable influence over foreign and military policy — control over Syria policy is a good example.	Governments still normally enjoy a Commons majority, after a brief pause in 2010–15.
Select committees are increasingly influential and have come under greater backbench control. They have forced government to reconsider such issues as bank regulation, attacking tax avoidance and evasion and procurement of equipment for the armed forces.	The government still relies on a large 'payroll vote' where all ministers, numbering more than 100, are bound by collective responsibility.
The Liaison Committee calls the prime minister increasingly to account. It is a more effective method than Prime Minister's Questions every week.	Government still controls the legislative programme and the **public bill** committees which propose amendments.
There were no decisive majorities for government between 2010 and 2017.	Prime ministerial patronage still creates loyalty among the government's own MPs.
The House of Lords has become increasingly proactive and obstructive. This is especially true when opposition in the Commons is weak, as occurred after 2015.	Government still has a huge advantage in resources (advice and research) over Members of Parliament.

Public bill A legislative proposal introduced into Parliament by the government. It becomes an Act of Parliament, and therefore law, if it passes all its legislative stages.

Exam tip

When discussing Parliament and its relationship with the executive, remember to consider both the House of Commons and the House of Lords.

Exam tip

Remember that the relationship between Parliament and the executive is not a static model; it is constantly changing according to circumstances. The most important circumstances include the size of the government's majority, the strength and unity of the government and the strength of opposition.

Now test yourself

3 Look at these issues concerning the relationship between the executive and Parliament in the UK. How do they affect the relationship?
   - Party whips
   - Collective responsibility
   - The doctrine of the mandate
   - Public Accounts Committee
   - Salisbury Convention
   - Parliament Acts

Answers on p. 128

The nature of the European Union

REVISED

There are four main features of the European Union:
- It is a customs union. This means that there are no tariffs (import taxes) on any goods and services being traded between member states. It also means that member states cannot have separate trade agreements with countries outside the EU. All external trade agreements are common to all members.
- It is a free market. This means there can be no barriers to the free movement of goods, services, finance, labour or people between member states. Citizens of a member state are also citizens of the European Union and can live wherever they wish within the Union and, broadly speaking, enjoy common citizenship rights.
- It is a partial political union. There are laws made by the institutions of the European Union which apply throughout the Union. These mostly relate to trade, consumer protection, development and agricultural subsidies, employment rights and production regulations. These laws ensure that all members compete on a level playing field using the same laws. It also means that the EU collects revenue from members and distributes it in the form of development aid, largely for agricultural and infrastructure development in poorer parts of the EU.
- Some but not all member states are part of a monetary union. This means they use the same currency, the euro.

In addition, the European Union was based on **four freedoms**:
- free movement of people within the EU
- free movement of labour within the EU
- free movement of capital (finance) within the EU
- free movement of goods and services within the EU.

The main areas of EU policy that will come under scrutiny after the UK's exit are as follows:
- Employment rights currently under the Social Chapter — the UK government must decide which such rights to retain and which to abandon.

Four freedoms [of the EU] Freedom of people, of labour, of capital and of goods and services. The EU is based on these principles and they are the subject of negotiation as the UK leaves the EU.

Exam practice answers and quick quizzes at **www.hoddereducation.co.uk/myrevisionnotesdownloads**

- Immigration policy from outside the EU — will the UK make stricter rules than those demanded by the EU?
- The **Common Agricultural Policy** uses a range of subsidies and regulations to control agricultural development. The principal question is whether the UK government will retain the subsidies and regulations.
- The **Common Fisheries Policy** is a series of regulations over fishing designed to conserve fish stocks and to ensure equal access to fishing among member states. After leaving the EU the UK government must decide how it will protect fishing and fish stocks in the national interest.

Exam tip

You will not be required to explain the operation of the European Union in any detail. However, in explaining the significance of the UK's exit, it is important to understand the principles of the EU, the four freedoms and the way in which sovereignty was divided between the UK and the EU.

Common Agricultural Policy A series of rules, regulations and subsidies designed to protect farmers from fluctuating market prices, to stabilise food prices and to encourage agricultural development and environmental protection. It is highly controversial as it eats up vast amounts of resources and may help inefficient farmers.

Common Fisheries Policy A series of regulations that ensures that all countries have a fair share of fishing grounds and are designed to protect fish stocks against over-fishing.

The constitutional impact of the UK leaving the European Union

REVISED

The following changes will occur in relation to the UK Constitution:
- The UK will regain all its national and legal sovereignty.
- The European Court of Justice will no longer have any jurisdiction in the UK and will cease to be the highest court of appeal on EU matters.
- There will be, for some time, a conflict over who should approve any future agreements with the European Union — should it be the UK Parliament, the elected government of the day or the people (in a referendum)?
- There may be constitutional implications for Scotland in particular. There remains a constitutional question whether the devolved Scottish government could have a different agreement with the EU than the rest of the UK.
- There is a problem in Northern Ireland concerning relations with the Republic of Ireland. If there is a closed border after the UK leaves the EU, it will cause problems over sovereignty on the island of Ireland.

Revision activity

Revise the following key issues:
1 How sovereignty will change when the UK leaves the EU.
2 At least two powers the government will regain when the UK leaves the EU.
3 Two EU bodies that will no longer control events in the UK when the UK leaves the EU.

The political impact of the UK leaving the European Union

REVISED

The following changes may occur in UK politics as a result of the UK's exit:
- There is a new political conflict concerning whether the UK should remain within the European single market.
- There is continuing conflict over whether there should be free movement of labour into and out of the UK. This conflict is both *within* and *between* parties.
- Immigration will probably remain a key political issue for many years to come.
- There may be an increasing divide between Scotland and the rest of the UK over relations with Europe.

- It may well see a dominant prime minister in Theresa May as she will be largely responsible for negotiating with the EU.
- UK government and Parliament will, for many years potentially, become preoccupied with how many current EU laws and regulations should be retained and transferred into UK law. The main areas for consideration are likely to be employment rights, fisheries policy and agricultural subsidies.

Now test yourself

TESTED

4 Look at the following features concerning the European Union. In each case describe how they affected the UK and what is likely to happen after the UK leaves the EU.
- The Social Chapter
- Free movement of people
- The Common Agricultural Policy
- The Common Fisheries Policy

Answers on p. 128

Legal and political sovereignty

REVISED

Legal sovereignty means:
- ultimate legal power
- no other body or institution can overrule Parliament, which has legal sovereignty
- legal sovereignty is fixed in one place unless the constitution is amended in some way to move it
- the courts will enforce only laws passed by the UK Parliament and will uphold only powers granted by the UK Parliament.

Political sovereignty:
- refers to where power lies *in reality* — although we know the UK Parliament is legally sovereign, we have to understand that *real* power may lie elsewhere
- may move according to changing circumstances
- is power which is not entrenched but which will be difficult to move to other bodies.

The changing location of sovereignty in the UK

REVISED

The key facts are these:
- **Legal sovereignty** lies with the UK Parliament.
- While the UK was a member of the European Union, some legal sovereignty was delegated to the EU.
- Although this appears to be a change in legal sovereignty, ultimately parliamentary sovereignty was not lost permanently because the UK had the option to leave the EU and restore all sovereignty. This is what has happened.
- **Political sovereignty** has moved to the devolved administrations.
- Some of the political sovereignty of the executive is shifting towards the UK Parliament. This is particularly true in the areas of foreign interventions and negotiation of foreign treaties.

> **Typical mistake**
>
> The Queen is often described as 'the sovereign'. This does not mean she exercises any sovereignty — the monarchy is politically and constitutionally inactive.

- The increasing use of referendums has transferred political sovereignty to the people.
- The prime minister has lost control over the date of general elections under the Fixed-term Parliaments Act.
- The Human Rights Act shifted control over the enforcement of rights from the UK Parliament to the Supreme Court.

Where sovereignty now lies in the UK

REVISED

The location of political sovereignty depends on circumstances:
- In a referendum the people are sovereign even though, technically, the result of a referendum is not binding on Parliament.
- At a general election the people are sovereign because they determine who shall exercise power for five years and to whom they are willing to grant a **mandate**.
- For issues which are part of the government's electoral mandate, it can be said the government is sovereign because it has popular consent for what it is doing.
- With devolved issues, the devolved administrations are effectively sovereign as it is unthinkable that they would be overruled by the UK Parliament.
- When implementing the European Convention on Human Rights, the Supreme Court becomes sovereign.

Mandate Authority granted by one body to another body to carry out certain actions and to make decisions. The most common usage of the term is when the people grant a mandate to the government by electing a particular party with a particular manifesto.

Revision activity

Make sure you thoroughly revise the following issues related to sovereignty:
1 Four possible locations of political sovereignty.
2 The key distinctions between legal and political sovereignty.
3 Three basic principles of parliamentary sovereignty.

Now test yourself

TESTED

5 Look at the bodies listed in the left column. In each case state the circumstances when they may be considered to be sovereign (there may be more than one circumstance).

Description	When sovereign
The Scottish Parliament	
The elected UK government	
The people	
The Supreme Court	
The European Court of Human Rights	

Answers on p. 128

Exam practice

AS

1 Describe the main functions of the Supreme Court. [10]
2 Describe the main features of judicial review. [10]
3 Using the source, explain the constitutional impact of the
  UK leaving the European Union. [10]

The decision by the UK to leave the European Union by 2019 is probably the most significant constitutional development in the UK for centuries. The treaties of the EU, notably of Rome and Maastricht, gradually drained sovereignty away from the UK and brought UK government and politics increasingly under the control of Brussels. The position of the European Court of Justice was especially controversial as it frequently made judgments that forced the UK government to adopt practices it had previously resisted. There was also disquiet over the role of Brussels bureaucrats who are neither elected nor accountable and yet appeared to be making policy. The sovereignty of Parliament seemed to have gone out of the window. Fortunately, this applied only to those areas of policy that had been transferred to Brussels in the treaties. It has to be said that large areas of policy have always remained within the control of UK government and Parliament.

Outside the EU the UK will regain all its sovereignty and the Supreme Court will once again be the highest court of appeal. The UK Parliament will no longer have to consider the European dimension when passing legislation. Meanwhile, civil servants and other policy makers will no longer be able to contribute to European legislation. All this, however, depends upon the nature of any agreement that the UK government may make with the EU after departure in March 2019.

Source: original material

In your response you must use knowledge and understanding to analyse points that are only in the source. You will **not** be rewarded for introducing any additional points that are not in the source.
4 'The UK Parliament is no longer sovereign.' How far do you agree with this view? [30]

A-level

1 Evaluate the extent to which the executive can control the UK Parliament. [30]
2 Evaluate the extent to which the Supreme Court can protect human rights
  in the UK. [30]
3 Using the source, evaluate the extent to which the UK judiciary can control
  executive power. [30]

The key reality of UK government and politics is that the UK Parliament is sovereign. This also means that Parliament is 'omnicompetent'. It can pass any legislation it wishes, however repugnant it may be, however unpopular it may prove and however much it may threaten human rights in the country. The lack of a codified constitution and a court that can overturn parliamentary legislation (in contrast to the powerful US Supreme Court) ensures the sovereignty of Parliament. Indeed, in the fight against terrorism, the UK government and Parliament have been forced to pass some legislation — for example, allowing the lengthy detention of terrorist suspects without trial — which threatens human rights.

Yet this view of the relationship between the Supreme Court and the UK Parliament is somewhat misleading. The *political* reality is rather different. Almost every time the Supreme Court has made an important judgment and constitutional declaration, the government and Westminster have, in fact, accepted the decision. The *Miller* case of 2016–17 was a case in point. The government had to introduce a motion to approve the UK's departure from the EU and MPs and peers fell into line. Similarly, whenever the rights of citizens are being considered by the senior judges, the government usually backs down. On some occasions an adverse decision can, of course, be reversed by introducing parliamentary legislation. In 2010, for example, the then chancellor Gordon Brown's 2005 decision to freeze the assets of terrorist suspects was outlawed by the Supreme Court. Accepting the decision, Brown promptly asked Westminster to grant him the power to do just that. The UK Parliament thus prevailed.

By contrast, however, when the Supreme Court ruled in 2011 that the DNA records of people who had not been convicted of a crime could not be held by the police, the government gave in and accepted the ruling, which was on the grounds that it offended the right to privacy.

The evidence is therefore contradictory. It all seems to come down to political considerations. The courts clearly have great authority, but government can often fall back on parliamentary sovereignty to get its way.

Source: original material

In your response you must:
● compare the different opinions in the source
● consider this view and the alternative to this view in a balanced way
● use knowledge and understanding to help you analyse and evaluate.

Answers and quick quiz 8 online

ONLINE

Summary

You should now have an understanding of:
● the role of the Supreme Court
● Supreme Court judgments — you will need to be able to quote several important ones
● the importance of judicial neutrality and independence
● how rights are protected in the UK
● how the senior judiciary can control executive power
● the principles of *ultra vires* and judicial review — you will also need to be able to quote some

examples to illustrate your understanding of the two concepts
● how the UK leaving the EU will affect the constitution and the politics of the UK
● the relationship between Parliament and government
● the extent to which the executive controls the UK Parliament
● how Parliament can control executive power
● the concept of sovereignty and the different types of sovereignty
● the changing location of sovereignty in the UK.

Now test yourself answers

Chapter 1

1

Democratic problem	Proposed remedy (remedies)
Part of the legislature is not accountable.	Introduce an elected second chamber.
The representation of parties in Parliament is distorted.	Introduce a proportional electoral system.
There are often low turnouts at elections.	Introduce compulsory voting.
There is a participation crisis in the UK.	Teach more citizenship in schools.

2 1 Use of referendums. 2 Constitutional changes require the use of referendums. 3 Results of referendums are politically binding.

3 1 Many parties may compete for power. 2 Power is widely dispersed. 3 Different views, beliefs and lifestyles are tolerated.

4

Form of representation	Individual or body
Representing the interests of a locality	Local councils, MPs
Representing the national interest	Both Houses of Parliament
Representing the interests of a particular section of society	Pressure groups
Representing the interests of a social class	Political parties

5 1 There is an elected legislature. 2 There are political parties. 3 Government is accountable to Parliament and/or the people.

6

Description	Example
An organisation that seeks to mobilise public opinion through the use of mass demonstrations	Friends of the Earth, 'peace' movements, occupational groups
An organisation that operates on behalf of business and seeks to influence ministers and parliamentarians directly	Confederation of British Industry (CBI) Institute of Directors (IOD)
An organisation that tends to use illegal methods or civil disobedience to gain public attention	Greenpeace, anti-fox hunting groups
An organisation that has local concerns and typically uses social media to organise protest	Anti-fracking, anti-airport expansion
An organisation that uses insider status to represent the interests of a particular section of society	National Farmers' Union, UK Finance

7 1 Parties seek governmental power, pressure groups do not. 2 Parties are accountable, pressure groups are not. 3 Parties adopt a wide range of policies, pressure groups have narrow concerns

8

Purpose	Development (with date if applicable)
A piece of legislation guaranteeing a wide range of rights and liberties	Human Rights Act 1998
A piece of legislation giving citizens access to official documents and information	Freedom of Information Act 2000
The creation of a body which can act as the highest level of appeal when citizens feel their rights may have been abused or ignored	Supreme Court 2005

Purpose	Development (with date if applicable)
A historical phenomenon stretching back centuries that guarantees anciently held rights	Common law
A device that helps citizens to appeal against unfair or unequal treatment by public bodies	Judicial review
A piece of legislation outlawing discrimination against women and minorities	Equality Act 2010

9 1 The European Convention on Human Rights.
   2 Judicial precedents (common law).
   3 Parliamentary statutes.

Chapter 2

1

Policy	Left wing, right wing or centrist?
The nationalisation of the railways	Left wing
The raising of the minimum wage well above the rate of inflation or the increase in earnings	Left wing
Reducing the rate of corporation tax levied on businesses	Right wing
Extending the rights of workers against unfair employment practices	Left wing
Extending the construction of nuclear power stations	Centrist
Increasing the level at which people start paying inheritance tax to £1 million	Right wing
Transferring local authority services into the private sector	Right wing

2 ● Right wing: 1 Selling off Royal Mail to private investors. 2 Increasing typical prison sentences for offenders.

● Left wing: 1 A wealth tax imposed on the very rich. 2 Building subsidised housing.

3

Policy	Party or parties
The introduction of more selective grammar schools	Conservative
The cancellation of the Trident nuclear missile renewal programme	Green Party
The reunification of Ireland	Sinn Fein
The abolition of university tuition fees	Labour
The introduction of proportional representation for general elections	Liberal Democrats
An extensive programme of infrastructure projects funded by government borrowing	Labour
Strict controls on immigration into the UK	UKIP

4 1 An extra rate of tax of 60% on those with very high incomes. 2 Cancellation of future building of nuclear power stations. 3 Cancellation of the HS2 — high-speed rail — project.

5 ● Conservative Party: introduction of more selective grammar schools (since abandoned); changes in the arrangements for people paying for social care to allow payments to be made after death; expansion of Heathrow airport.
● Labour Party: abolition of university tuition fees; large infrastructure projects funded by government borrowing; new higher rate of tax on very high-income groups.
● Liberal Democratic Party: referendum on the Brexit deal with the European Union; extensive house-building programme; introduction of an elected second chamber in Parliament.
● UKIP: strict controls on future immigration; introduction of grammar schools; reductions in taxes on business.
● Scottish National Party: consideration of a second independence referendum (since abandoned); further investment in renewable energy; special arrangements for Scotland following Brexit.

6 *Daily Telegraph* — Conservative. *Daily Mail* — Conservative. *Daily Mirror* — Labour. *Guardian* — Labour/Liberal Democrat. *Sun* — Conservative.

Chapter 3

1
- The mandate: makes a new government legitimate.
- Legitimacy: governments need to win elections to enjoy democratic legitimacy.
- Accountability: at elections the outgoing government is accountable to the people.
- Representation: elections ensure that constituents are fully represented.

2
- Proportionality: PR gives more proportional outcomes than first-past-the-post.
- Voter choice: some systems such as STV and AMS give voters more than one vote.
- Equal value of votes: under pure PR systems every vote counts equally.
- Small parties: small parties are more likely to win seats under PR.
- Democratic legitimacy: parties or coalitions which win under PR can claim a genuine consensus of support.

3

Description	Electoral system
An electoral system that regularly produced a government with a working majority in the UK Parliament until 2010	First-past-the-post
An electoral system that allows voters to discriminate between candidates of the same party	STV
An electoral system that ensures that the winner is supported by a majority of voters	SV
An electoral system that gives voters two votes	AMS
An electoral system that features both constituencies and proportional representation	AMS

4 The differential top-up system gives a disproportionately large number of seats under the regional list system to those parties that are most significantly discriminated against in the first-past-the-post part of the system.

5

Description	Example
A party won many more seats than its proportion of the popular vote warranted.	In 2015 the Conservatives won more than 50% of the seats with 38% of the national vote.
A party won only one seat but won a considerable proportion of the popular vote.	UKIP in 2015.
A party whose representation at Westminster was all but wiped out.	The Liberal Democrats in 2015 lost all but eight of their seats.
A party won a parliamentary majority by winning only about one third of the popular vote.	Labour in 2005.

Chapter 4

1
- 2015
- 2015
- 2010
- 1992

2
- The young
- 65+
- DE
- C2
- 18–34

3

Description	What is being described
A general term for the party image and competence as it affects voting support	Valence
The increasing tendency for people not to consider themselves part of a particular social class or to adopt the typical attitudes associated with that class	Class dealignment

Exam practice answers and quick quizzes at **www.hoddereducation.co.uk/myrevisionnotesdownloads**

Description	What is being described
The increasing tendency for people not to consider themselves closely attached to one particular party and its policies	Partisan dealignment
The name given to the idea that a party that wins an election has the democratic authority to carry out its manifesto commitments	Mandate

4
- The young.
- Lower-income groups.
- Members of ethnic minorities.

5

Opinion poll forecast	Likely impact
They forecast a landslide victory for one party.	People may be reluctant to vote for that party to avoid an over-powerful party.
They predict a hung parliament.	People will vote for the party they think is most likely to win to avoid a coalition.
They predict a very close result.	Many people may vote tactically.
They predict that an extreme right-wing party will do well.	They may be inclined to vote Conservative.
They predict that an extreme left-wing party will do well.	They may be tempted to vote Liberal Democrat.

Chapter 5

1

Constitutional source	Examples	
Parliamentary statute	Human Rights Act	Freedom of Information Act
	Parliament Acts	Equality Act
Work of authority	Bagehot's English Constitution	Blackstone's Commentaries

Constitutional source	Examples	
Convention	Salisbury Convention	Collective responsibility
Common law and tradition	Freedom of association	Freedom of speech
External treaty or agreement	Maastricht Treaty 1992	NATO

2 Countries with a codified constitution: USA, Germany, France, Spain, Russia, Japan, many others. Countries without a codified constitution: Israel, New Zealand.

3

Reform	Government
Human Rights Act	Labour 1997–2001
Fixed-term Parliaments Act	Conservative 2010–15
Constitutional Reform Act	Labour 2001–05
House of Lords Act	Labour 1997–2001
Freedom of Information Act	Labour 1997–2001
English Votes for English Laws Order	Conservative 2010–15

4 House of Lords Act, Fixed-term Parliaments Act, Recall of MPs Act.

5

Power	Countries
Health care administration	Scotland, Wales, Northern Ireland
Criminal laws	Scotland, Northern Ireland
Income tax levels	Scotland
Education	Scotland, Wales, Northern Ireland

6 It can raise or lower the rate of income tax and decide how to use revenue from income tax. It also has control over a variety of other minor taxes.

Chapter 6

1

Power	Who is being described
An MP who presides over debates in the House of Commons	The Speaker
A party official who seeks to ensure that MPs or peers representing a party vote according to the wishes of the party leadership	A party whip
An appointed member in the House of Lords who does not have any party allegiance	Crossbencher
The person, a member of the opposition, who presides over a committee that examines the financial arrangements of the government	Chair of the Public Accounts Committee

2 To investigate the financial arrangements of government and to ensure taxpayers get good value for money.

3 ● Scrutiny: examining proposed legislation and suggesting amendments.
● Supply days: days when debates are chosen by the opposition parties.
● Vote of no confidence: when Parliament votes on whether the government should continue in office.
● Committee stage: Parliament considers possible amendments to legislation.
● Second reading: the main debate on the principles of a piece of legislation.

4

Description	Principle or convention
A rule guaranteeing the rights of MPs to say whatever they wish without fear of prosecution or being sued for defamation.	Parliamentary privilege
The House of Lords must not obstruct proposals which were contained in the governing party's last election manifesto.	Salisbury Convention
The House of Lords can only delay government legislation for one year.	Parliament Act

Description	Principle or convention
A brief opportunity for backbench MPs to raise a special issue on the floor of the House	Ten-minute rule

5 House of Commons — bill committees, departmental select committees, Public Accounts Committee. House of Lords — bill committees.

6

Parliamentary activity	Institution which carries it out
Examining the work of government departments	Departmental select committees
Delaying legislation for at least one year	House of Lords
Scrutiny of legislation by the whole House	House of Lords committee stage
Debating great issues largely free of party control	Free vote
Examining the effectiveness of the government's financial arrangements	Public Accounts Committee

7 Critically examine the policies of government departments. Operate largely free of party control. Members are elected by backbench MPs.

Chapter 7

1

Power	Limitations
To appoint or dismiss ministers	He or she may be forced to appoint important party figures even against their preference.
To conduct foreign policy	Parliament may overrule the government.
To control cabinet	Cabinet may outvote the prime minister.
To make government policy	He or she must carry the support of parliament.
To call a general election	He or she needs the approval of two-thirds of the House of Commons.

2 Individual ministerial responsibility requires a minister to face criticism or even resign if a major error is made by their department. Collective responsibility requires that all members of the government should defend government policy or resign or face dismissal.

3

Description	What is being described
The doctrine that a government minister should resign if their department makes a serious mistake	Individual ministerial responsibility
A convention that allows the prime minister to exercise the arbitrary powers of the monarch	Prerogative powers
The power of the prime minister that derives from their power over ministerial appointments and dismissals	Patronage
A subdivision of the cabinet where many policies are worked out in detail	Cabinet committees
The civil servant who helps the prime minister to manage the cabinet	Cabinet secretary

4 Patronage. Negotiating foreign treaties. Commander-in-chief.

5

Description	Prime minister	Details
He or she resigned after losing a referendum vote.	David Cameron	In 2016.
He or she became prime minister without fighting a general election.	Gordon Brown	Following the resignation of Tony Blair.
	Theresa May	Following the resignation of David Cameron.
He or she was forced to fight a leadership contest after losing support for a key policy.	Margaret Thatcher	In 1990 following opposition to her poll tax policy.

Description	Prime minister	Details
He or she resigned in favour of a rival from within their own party.	Tony Blair	In favour of Gordon Brown.
He or she lost a general election after governing for seven years.	John Major	Prime minister 1990–97, lost an election to Labour.

6 David Cameron had resigned as Conservative leader after he lost the EU referendum. A party leadership election followed and all Theresa May's rivals dropped out one by one.

Chapter 8

1

Description	What is being described
The legal principle involved when a public body is accused of acting beyond its statutory powers	*Ultra vires*
The principle that judges must not be influenced by government when considering legal cases	Judicial independence
The principle that judges should not display any obvious political allegiance	Judicial neutrality
A legal case which is judging whether an action by a public body was fair, within legal powers, was the result of proper procedures and/or treated citizens equally	Judicial review
The constitutional principle that all citizens, including government, should be treated equally under the law	The rule of law

2 By conducting judicial reviews of government decisions. By implementing the terms of the European Convention on Human Rights. By implementing constitutional rules and restrictions.

3
- Party whips: help to maintain party discipline and ensure MPs vote according to the wishes of the leadership.
- Collective responsibility: ensures the government presents a unified image.
- The doctrine of the mandate: gives a government the democratic legitimacy to implement its manifesto commitments.
- Public Accounts Committee: investigates the government's financial arrangements and may be critical of how public money is spent.
- Salisbury Convention: prevents the House of Lords from blocking government proposals for which it has an electoral mandate.
- Parliament Acts: limit the powers of the House of Lords. The Lords can only delay legislation for one year and has no control over financial matters.

4
- The Social Chapter: this forced the UK government to implement various employment protection measures.
- Free movement of people: citizens of EU countries can enter or leave the UK at will.
- The Common Agricultural Policy: establishes various environmental protections, grants various subsidies to farmers and maintains price controls over produce.

- The Common Fisheries Policy: establishes restrictions on fishing to protect fish stocks and ensure fair sharing of fishing rights among member countries.

5

Description	When sovereign
The Scottish Parliament	When setting the rate of income tax. When establishing criminal and civil law in Scotland.
The elected UK government	When it has a clear electoral mandate to implement certain policies.
The people	At a referendum.
The Supreme Court	When imposing the terms of the European Convention on Human Rights.
The European Court of Human Rights	When hearing an appeal based on the European Convention on Human Rights.